CARL MARTIN

HEAVEN

Think On These Things

TGP

Total Grace Publications
Santa Clarita, California

Total Grace Publications is a Christian publishing company dedicated to the production and distribution of quality Christian books, video tapes, and audio tapes which teach and proclaim the grace freely offered by Jesus Christ. We believe that this is more than partial grace, providing forgiveness alone; it is total grace, which includes Christ's imparted power to overcome. It is in this spirit that we ask God's blessing upon you as you read this book.

—the Publishers

Cover design by Kathleen Thorne-Thomsen

ISBN 0-9665935-0-2

Library of Congress Catalog Card Number: 99-90538

All texts are taken from the
Authorized King James Version

Total Grace Publications
28010 N. Tiffany Ln. #302
Santa Clarita, California 91351
www.totalgrace.com

For Coleen:
My girlfriend, best
friend, and wife.
You make my world
a little bit of heaven.

The events described in this book pertain to both heaven and the new earth, and the terms are used interchangeably. Chronologically speaking, they all take place after the great Resurrection at the Second Coming. Christians have long debated what happens on earth during the "one thousand years" spoken of in Revelation 20 (referred to by many as "the Millennium"). Although the Bible is quite clear on this matter, and will make the truth known to all who study prayerfully and with a teachable spirit, we do not address the issue in this writing. The chapters entitled "Strange Fire" and "Behold All Things New" cover events occurring just after the Millennium, when the New Jerusalem (heaven) comes down to earth, but other than that, little mention is given to the subject. I highly recommend the **Discover Bible School* Bible studies for anyone who wishes to learn more about this and other Bible prophecies. That there will be a new earth is confirmed by the writings of Isaiah, Peter, and John (see Isaiah 65:17; 66:22; 2 Peter 3:13; Revelation 21:1).

One area that is not particularly clear in the Bible is the extent of our relationships with each other in heaven and the new earth. Jesus said in Matthew 22:30 that "in the resurrection they neither marry, nor are given in marriage." His point was that if a man dies and his wife remarries, she will not necessarily have to choose one with whom to spend eternity while breaking the other's heart. On the other hand, as one pastor put it, we shouldn't be insistent that when the Lord returns He will give every happy couple their divorce papers. The fact is, we don't really have a lot of biblical information on this issue. It is for this reason that all of the redeemed in this writing are portrayed as individuals enjoying various activities as opposed to doing so as married couples. Christ's words are quite plain, but we still do not know exactly how we will relate to one another in that glorious land. As Christians we should always trust that whatever God has planned, it will be better than we can imagine. It is quite safe to say that no one will be disappointed when they get there.

While certain subjects herein are definitely detailed in Scripture (the dimensions of the City, the fact that we will build houses, the truth about hell, etc.) others are merely implied in Scripture and fall into the category of "eye hath not seen" and "with God all things are possible" (flying like angels, inner space study, exploring the galaxies, etc.). In either case, the main purpose is to get the reader to understand that our God is a God of endless creativity and limitless possibilities. While we should not speculate as to the definite details of such activities and call them a sure thing, we need to be equally cautious of renouncing them simply because "eye hath not seen." Otherwise the mind will focus on earthly things and forget that God does indeed have something better which is as real as the ground on which you stand.

In keeping with the King James translation, all pronouns of the Deity are quoted in lower case. However, all commentary and narration render these words in upper case as a gesture of reverence and respect.

I am under no delusion that I have gleaned all there is to say about the home of the redeemed. One of the things I am most looking forward to is seeing just how far short all of my imaginings fall. However big I describe it, think bigger. However bright, think brighter. However glorious, think more glorious. No matter what image comes to mind, remember that it hasn't even entered into your heart what God has prepared for them that love Him.

**Available in the back of this book. -Publishers*

CONTENTS

FOREWORD

Carl Martin is a wordsmith. An artist, really. When he sent me his preliminary draft for this book on "Heaven" I was eager to lay eyes on the manuscript. There was a secret reason why I was so intrigued, albeit a somewhat selfish one. I had heard about Carl and his insatiable quest to make it big in Hollywood by writing. Frankly, I couldn't wait to take the document with me aboard my scheduled airline trip en route to a speaking engagement. As I settled back into my seat, I wondered half aloud, How can someone whose life has changed so dramatically from sinner to saint handle a sacred topic like heaven? Can an aspiring Hollywood writer and producer avoid the slick stuff? Will this have the glitzy glitter of sleazy Tinseltown? Or speak to my heart?

Words have a powerful effect on our lives. And I must tell you that before I immersed myself into the third chapter of the transcripts, Carl's words began to work on me. I was in for a pleasant journey full of spiritual surprises. "This stuff reads like biblical fiction," I mused half-aloud. Fascinating. Thrilling insights! Yet carefully and painstakingly researched and backed up with solid Scripture. Its pages read almost like a modern prophet—although Carl would be the first to vigorously deny any such categorization.

Yet, why not? That is partly what the prophetic gift is all about, isn't it? Prophecy is simply the practical exposition of Scripture in new and dynamic ways. Timely. Other-worldly. Heavenly.

So stick with this guy, as I did. You will be glad you did. I know you are busy. So was I. But you will discover that eating blueberry pie à la mode in heaven would be sheer punishment (due to lack of flavor) compared with the main course at the wedding feast which chef Jesus has in mind to serve you. Every believer in Jesus Christ will be challenged and inspired by this powerful, instructive devotional book on the eternal home of the saved.

E. Lonnie Melashenko
Moorpark, California
February 15, 1999

In a world full of sin, misery, and selfishness, a wise prophet calls our attention away from the world and directs us to better things. With keen spiritual insight and under the direction of the Holy Spirit, the apostle Paul admonishes us:

"Finally brethren, whatsoever things are true, whatsoever things are honest, whatsoever things are just, whatsoever things are pure, whatsoever things are lovely, whatsoever things are of good report; if there be any virtue, and if there be any praise, think on these things" (Philippians 4:8).

Just as "we are what we eat" nutritionally speaking, so in our spiritual life we are what we behold and contemplate. Scripture declares:

"But we all...beholding...are changed into the same image" (2 Corinthians 3:18).

"For as he thinketh in his heart, so is he" (Proverbs 23:7).

These are not just good suggestions. They are laws: unchangeable, inevitable. When God says something, it happens. But they are more than laws, they are promises. These give us hope that by dwelling upon spiritual things that are true, honest, just, pure, and lovely we will be transformed into the same image.

"Whereby are given unto us exceeding great and precious promises: that by these ye might be partakers of the divine nature" (2 Peter 1:4).

We are living in a time of earth's history unparalleled in its propagation of *un*true, *dis*honest, *un*just, *im*pure, and *un*lovely things to behold. It is the *bad* report that tops the headlines. "Virtue" is sadly lacking in the media and entertainment industries, and there seems to be very little godly "praise" around us. Indeed we are surrounded by an atmosphere diametrically opposed to that which Paul prescribed. Our senses can be bombarded with such things throughout the day and into the night: the newspaper in the morning, the radio and billboards on the way to work, the pictures and gossip in the workplace, the television before dinner, the Internet after dinner, and perhaps the captivating novel just before bed.

And yet amidst all of this there is an alternate route, a wonderful road upon which to travel. "Thou wilt show me the path of life" (Psalm 16:11). This path is the one that leads to, and abides in the Savior. It is the path of a more abundant life, filled with freedom, joy, and peace (see John 10:10; 8:32; 15:11; 14:27).

The same apostle that called us to think upon holy things, boldly declared his favorite theme for contemplation:

"I count all things but loss for the excellency of the knowledge of Jesus Christ my Lord" (Philippians 3:8).

This book is not about a place so much as a Person. It is written with the hope that all who read it may obtain such a living knowledge of the Redeemer that they will count all things but loss in comparison to that wonderful, abiding relationship.

It is my sincere prayer that this little book bring you into a closer walk with your Creator, by leading you not only through a journey of tomorrow, but to the foot of the old, rugged Cross. May you come to realize that the greatest thrill awaiting you is not the mansions, or the miracles, or the trips to galaxies afar, but rather the face to face encounters you will have with your Savior. Heaven is "true," it is "pure," and it is "lovely." But most of all it is your future home, to be shared with the One whose very name is "Love." No wonder Paul directs us to "think on these things."

—Carl Martin

"I will come again, and receive you unto myself; that where I am, there ye may be also." —John 14:3

"For the Lord himself shall descend from heaven with a shout, with the voice of the archangel, and with the trump of God: and the dead in Christ shall rise first: Then we which are alive and remain shall be caught up together with them in the clouds to meet the Lord in the air: and so shall we ever be with the Lord."
—1 Thessalonians 4:16,17

Everything seems surreal. You have never seen a sky like this before. The clouds overhead look like mammoth black waves crashing violently against each other. The earth is trembling as if it too is aware of the approaching power. You have studied the Bible and have known for several years that you were living in the last days, but you always put the Second Coming a bit further into the future. Could this be it? Everyone around you seems to be wondering the same thing as they look up into the angry skies. Then your eye catches it; way up over the eastern sky you notice a tiny, dark cloud. It gradually grows larger and brighter as it slowly moves toward earth. Now you begin to make out the shapes within the cloud. You are mesmerized by the scene. Chills run down your spine in joyous anticipation of the awesome event. You think you see people way off in the cloud, but it's hard to tell from such a distance. Each appears to be holding something gold, and now you see they also possess what look like wings. These are *angels*—innumerable angels—each holding a golden trumpet! You know that the greatest event in the history of the universe is now taking place, and you still cannot believe it! So long talked about, so long contemplated, and now it is happening!

Many of those around you are horror-stricken by the scene. They begin to wail in terror, and out of the corner of your eye you perceive that several have started to run away. Where they will go, you know not. All you know is this is your God, and you have waited for Him!

❖ ❖ ❖

There is a better land. By the authority of the One who created all things, there is a place that is prepared "for you." Before we continue our journey, let's find out a little more about that land and the promise to take you there. This promise was given by One who has never lied. He did not return to heaven after His resurrection only to forget about those of us on earth. He went to prepare a place for us—for you. Coupled with this promise is the assurance that He will come again. The reason He will come again is even more profound: so that where He is, *there you may be also*. He loves you. He wants to be with you. Like a parent who desires all of the children to be present at family get-togethers, so He desires that all will be present in His eternal kingdom. Heaven won't be the same without you.

So why the apparent delay? Why, if Christ is so eager to come back and take us home with Him, are we still here? The apostle Peter prophesied in regard to these things. He said, "Knowing this first, that there shall come in the last days scoffers, walking after their own lusts, And saying Where is the promise of his coming? for since the fathers fell asleep, all things continue as they were from the beginning of creation," "The Lord is not slack concerning his promise, as some men count slackness; but is longsuffering to us-ward, not willing that any should perish, but that all should come to repentance" (2 Peter 3:3,4,9).

Jesus loves every person on the earth today. He longs for each one of us to come to repentance and surrender ourselves to Him fully, for that is the only hope of salvation.

The Bible is clear as to what the Second Coming will look like:

"For as the lightning cometh out of the east, and shineth even unto the west; so shall also the coming of the Son of man be" (Matthew 24:27).

"When the Son of man shall come in his glory, and all the holy angels with him" (Matthew 25:31).

"Behold he cometh with clouds; and every eye shall see him" (Revelation 1:7).

This event will be like nothing human eyes have ever beheld. The King of all the universe, the One who created all things, is going to come down through the corridors of the sky accompanied by all of His angels. What a sight to behold! The glory surrounding a single angel is enough to overwhelm the senses (see Revelation 19:10; Luke 24:4,5). Just try to imagine what "ten thousand times ten thousand, and thousands of thousands" of them at once will look like (Revelation 5:11).

Graves will burst open on that day. "Behold, I shew you a mystery; We shall not all sleep, but we shall all be changed, In a moment, in the twinkling of an eye, at the last trump: for the trumpet shall sound, and the dead shall be raised incorruptible, and we shall be changed...then shall be brought to pass the saying that is written, Death is swallowed up in victory. O death, where is thy sting? O grave, where is thy victory?" (1 Corinthians 15:51,52,54,55).

Those alive for this event will be reunited with loved ones who had died, as these precious souls come forth from their graves. All who have believed on Christ and abided in Him will be safe from the power of death forevermore. Funerals will from that day forward be a thing of the past as the redeemed dwell in the presence of the one true Life-giver.

As the dead in Christ are resurrected, the bodies of the living will be transformed instantly into glorious, perfect bodies.

"For our conversation is in heaven; from whence also we look for the Savior, the Lord Jesus Christ: Who shall change our vile body, that it may be fashioned like unto his glorious body" (Philippians 3:20,21).

In a moment, in the "twinkling of an eye," we will be changed from the bodies we now have, into perfect, eternally youthful bodies, like that of our Lord.

It is the misconception of what heaven will be like, and what we will be like when we get there, that causes many to picture it as a boring place where we float around bodiless on clouds and strum harps. Such a concept makes heaven seem imaginary and unappealing. Thus the eyes of multitudes are focused on the pleasures of this world, for everything here seems so much more real. When Jesus comes again our bodies will transformed into actual, tangible, glorified bodies like His own.

All the faithful children of God will rejoice in victory as the glorious cloud, filled with angels and surrounding the Son of God, descends toward the earth.

"And it shall be said in that day, Lo, this is our God; we have waited for him, and he will save us: this is the Lord; we have waited for him, we will be glad and rejoice in his salvation" (Isaiah 25:9).

"And then shall appear the sign of the Son of man in heaven: and then shall all the tribes of the earth mourn, and they shall see the Son of man coming in the clouds of heaven with power and great glory. And he shall send his angels with a great sound of a trumpet, and they shall gather together his elect from the four winds, from one end of heaven to the other" (Matthew 24:30,31).

With that in mind, let's resume our contemplation of that wonderful day for which we so eagerly wait.

❖ ❖ ❖

Now the angels, although still a great way off, are becoming more defined, and the flames that cover the base of the cloud grow brighter as it descends. The angels raise their golden trumpets and shake the earth with a thunderous blast. In the center of the cloud, the glory of the King is finally unveiled, and His brightness outshines a thousand suns. Your best and most creative conceptions of this event have been completely eclipsed by the reality. You weren't aware that your senses could withstand such stimulus. But at the same time, you realize that your body, along with your senses, has been changed. You look down and notice a whole new physique, loaded with energy and vitality. No longer do you wear those man-made clothes that constantly have to be replaced. Now you are "clothed in white" as the book of Revelation said you would be. This "white robe," though, is not made from any material you have ever felt. It shines as did Moses' face when he had been with God on Mount Sinai. It looks as though it's made of pure light!

Now the cloud shines forth in all it's dazzling splendor, the Son of God in the middle, brightest of all. The army of angels stretches out for miles in all directions beneath the massive band of fire at the base of the cloud. Myriads of them descend toward the earth, spreading out in all directions. You witness several approach a hillside graveyard in the distance. The mighty voice of Jesus calls forth His faithful children.

Some of the graves burst open. These ransomed ones who died in the faith of Jesus now come forward in their glorified bodies. Their faces shine as do their robes, and many of them ecstatically hug and kiss each other, overwhelmed by the joyful reunion. The angels are right there beside them, and it appears they are telling them something. Suddenly you think of several loved ones who had died. You have longed to see them again and today is the day your dream will come true! One relative was buried close by, and you can't wait to see her.

But the King of the universe attracts your attention. His majesty and beauty are captivating to His children. No crown of thorns mars that perfect head now. He wears instead the glorious crown of the King of all Creation. You cannot stop looking at His wonderful face. It seems to be the very image of love.

Yet while His face shines with love to you, that same face strikes fear in the hearts of those who continually rejected the gentle promptings of His Holy Spirit. In the distance you hear the very words of another prophecy echoed in various ways: "Hide us from the face of him that sitteth on the throne, and from the wrath of the Lamb!" (Revelation 6:16).

Now the horizon is beginning to display white-robed multitudes rising up toward the spectacular cloud. These are the resurrected saints. The sky is just loaded with them, almost giving the appearance of countless stars. It is a magnificent sight.

The earth's surface all around you is broken up. Mountains have disappeared into the ground and all of humankind's proud skyscrapers have been leveled. The lordly palaces and mansions, so long coveted, are now heaps of wood, stone, metal, and brick. The earth still rumbles from violent aftershocks.

Suddenly you feel yourself being lifted off the ground by the unseen power of the Savior. An angel meets you in midair and accompanies you toward the glorious, mammoth cloud. The earth below and the plans of men are in ruins, but the Lord has not forgotten you. He has come again to receive you unto Himself, just as He promised.

The flaming base of the cloud blankets the sky just above you and extends as far as the eye can see. What will it be like to enter this holy place? Angels and people are shining all around you as they too advance toward their magnificent destination.

Your mind races in wild anticipation as you rise up above the cloud's edge and move over into its glorious body. This cloud is nothing like the fluffy white things that have filled the skies all your life. This one is made of something you've never seen before. And part of what gives it its shape are the shining angels themselves.

Jesus smiles even brighter as His precious children are moved in close to Him. As much as you and all of the redeemed have waited and longed for this moment, the Savior has yearned for it even more. Never again will He and His children be apart. He has prepared a place for them, and now He is taking them home.

As you gaze at the face of your Lord in admiration, you suddenly feel a hand on your shoulder. You turn around and there before you stands your relative who had been buried in your hometown! An angel had pointed you out to her as you came up over the edge of the cloud. The love that flows from the Son of God envelopes the two of you as you embrace and weep for joy. Just as you will never have to be separated from Jesus again, so you and this person will never have to say goodbye. The two of you now look back up to Christ as you begin to make your way toward His majestic form at the enormous cloud's center. No words need be spoken. The energy of love in this place is so powerful it can be felt.

The flaming cloud of glory now begins to back away from the desolate earth. Its mission has been accomplished and now it will head through the vast expanses of space toward heaven. What a trip awaits the redeemed! Everything they have ever known about science can be left back on earth now. Sin has not marred this otherwise perfect universe, for Satan has been cast to the earth. Nothing on this old world could have prepared you for the things your eyes are about to behold.

Wonder and amazement overtake you as you and your loved one watch the stars rush by at a tremendous speed. You don't understand the science behind the movement of this colossal cloud, nor does it matter to you. All is in Christ's hands, and with Him all things are possible. An angel reveals that you are on your way to the New Jerusalem and this sends new chills down your spine. You will soon be entering the Holy City of God in heaven!

You and your relative have other loved ones and friends somewhere aboard this tremendous cloud and you're anxious to see them as well. But for now your greatest desire is to press closer to Jesus. As you near His form, you see that He is overcome with joy. His children, His precious children who have willingly chosen Him over the Enemy, now surround Him. Of the faithful, not a single one is missing. His smile is understandable. Jesus sees before Him here, the fruit of His work. The pain, suffering and agony He went through on Calvary was for this very moment. As He beholds the beaming countenances of those who are now eternally secure through His blood, His face reveals that it was all well worth it to Him. This massive reunion of souls, this grand parade of the victorious, make His pain and suffering worthwhile. The angels strike a note higher, and sing the chorus of their powerful song:

"He shall see of the travail of his soul, and shall be satisfied" (Isaiah 53:11).

"God is not ashamed to be called their God: for he hath prepared for them a city." —Hebrews 11:16

Forget everything you know about cities. For most of us, the thought of a city is not exactly Paradise. Trash fills the streets, road repair and construction are constantly causing delays, the noise generates headaches, crime is a dilemma, and air pollution is almost a given. These cities, however, are built by humans. God has prepared a city for us with His own hands. In this city there will be no trash, no road repairs, no primitive machinery noise, no crime (for unconverted criminals will not be there: Matthew 6:20; Revelation 21:8), and not one impure particle in the air or water. The name of this city is the New Jerusalem (Revelation 21:1,2); the features of this city, incomparable.

THE SIZE

"The city lieth foursquare, and the length is as large as the breadth: and he measured the city with the reed, twelve thousand furlongs" (Revelation 21:16).

A furlong is one-eighth of a mile. If the city's perimeter is 12,000 furlongs, then it is 1,500 miles around. Since its length is as large as its breadth, then the city has a perfectly square perimeter 375 miles long on each side: one city, larger than the state of Oregon! We're also told in the same verse: "The length and the breadth and the height of it are equal." This seems to indicate that the Holy City is shaped much like a giant, golden cube, its height being equal to its length and breadth. Thus the top of the city would sit 375 miles above the base.

"*And he measured the wall thereof, an hundred and forty and four cubits*" (Revelation 21:16).

A cubit is 18 inches. The measurement expressed here is 216 feet. Some believe this is describing the *height* of the wall, which is a possibility. However, it seems much more likely that the wall is 216 feet *thick.* For one thing, if the city itself is an incredible 375 miles high, a wall rising 216 feet would seem far out of proportion—almost tiny. The prophet John, after seeing the enormous city in all of its grandeur, described the wall as "great and high" (Revelation 21:12): an unlikely phrase for such a relatively short wall. Another clue that the wall is probably higher than 216 feet can be found in the city's foundations.

"And the wall of the city had twelve foundations" (Revelation 21:14).

Notice it said, "the *wall* of the city had twelve foundations," not "the city had twelve foundations." Another text concurs:

"And the foundations of the wall of the city were garnished with all manner of precious stones" (Revelation 21:19).

Reading on, we find that each of the twelve foundations is made of a different precious stone. One thought on this is that these twelve foundations lie, one on top of the other, at the base of the city. Again, this is a possibility and should not be ruled out. But the wording seems to indicate that the foundations are separate, and connected to the walls themselves, not just stacked on each other. In other words, each foundation is a separate *floor* in this giant city, each floor equidistant from the others (more than 30 miles apart!). The language here implies that the New Jerusalem is one giant twelve-story structure that God has built for His children. In this case, the walls would by definition need to rise to the very top of the City.

"And the building of the wall of it was of jasper" (Revelation 21:18).

Jasper is an opaque, brilliant, green stone. This tells us that even though the wall stretches clear to the top of this metropolis, one can see inside all 12 floors by looking right through it. The word "Jasper" however, falls far short of the dazzling brilliance the wall will produce. Imagine this mammoth structure towering 375 miles overhead and shining with the glory of God's throne!

"The first foundation was jasper" (Revelation 21:19). The walls are made of the same material as the first or lowest foundation. This hints once again at the idea of each foundation being a different floor, having the first floor and walls forming the great structure on which everything else is built.

The other foundations are made from precious stones as well. Sapphire, chalcedony, emerald, sardonyx, sardius, chrysolyte, beryl, topaz, chrysoprasus, jacinth, and amethyst are used for the remaining 11 floors. If some of these gems are unfamiliar to you, rejoice; they'll be even more brilliant and glorious than you can imagine, no matter what they're called.

"And the wall of the city had twelve foundations, and in them the names of the twelve apostles of the Lamb" (Revelation 21:14).

Each foundation contains one of the names of the twelve apostles of Jesus. But why put their names in such a place? The Bible gives us the answer: "Now therefore ye are no more strangers and foreigners, but fellowcitizens with the saints, and of the household of God; And are built upon the foundation of the apostles and prophets, Jesus Christ himself being the chief corner stone" (Ephesians 2:20).

Jesus is the only rock upon whom we are to build our faith. But the words of the apostles and the truths they handed down to us are the way we become familiar with who Jesus is. To reject the words of these inspired men is to reject Christ Himself, for He speaks to us through the writings of the apostles and prophets. "Believe in the Lord your God, so shall ye be established; believe his prophets, so shall ye prosper" (2 Chronicles 20:20).

These twelve foundations testify to the validity and accuracy of the instruments through which God conveyed His Word. What a thrill it will be to walk on these transparent, glistening foundations! Believe His prophets now, and you will walk on their foundations then.

THE PEARLY GATES

"And the twelve gates were twelve pearls; every several gate was of one pearl" (Revelation 21:21).

For a city this size, these gates must be simply enormous. Now imagine each gate having the appearance of a lustrous pearl. The light from the throne of God will constantly flow out from the city and shimmer off each one of them.

"And had a wall great and high, and had twelve gates, and at the gates twelve angels, and names written thereon, which are the names of the twelve tribes of Israel: On the east three gates; on the north three gates; on the south three gates; and on the west three gates" (Revelation 21:12,13).

After Adam and Eve fell by partaking of the forbidden fruit, God sent the couple out of Eden and placed angels on the east end of the Garden to prevent them from returning to the Tree of Life (see Genesis 3:24). In the New Jerusalem, however, God places angels at the gates, not to keep mankind out, but rather to welcome them *in* to their eternal home. "And the gates of it shall not be shut at all by day: for there shall be no night there" (Revelation 21:25).

Upon each of these gates is written one of the names of the twelve tribes of Israel. Some of these names belong to men who had more than their share of failures. For all eternity these gates will bear witness to the fact that although frail and erring, repentant souls who seek the blood of Jesus Christ can not only find cleansing, but also transformation and ultimately victory in the life.

The material the Lord chose for the construction of these gates is no accident either. "Again, the kingdom of heaven is like unto a merchant man, seeking goodly pearls: Who, when he had found one pearl of great price, went and sold all that he had, and bought it" (Matthew 13:45,46).

The pearl of great price is Jesus Himself. Although salvation is a free gift, it is given only to those who have surrendered all to Him. Those who enter through these gates will have found the great pearl in their relationship with Christ, and will have given everything they are over to Him. Their talents, ambitions, opinions, even soul, body, and spirit, will have been consecrated fully to Him and His cause. "Then said Jesus unto his disciples, If any man will come after me, let him deny himself, and take up his cross and follow me," "I am crucified with Christ: nevertheless I live; yet not I, but Christ liveth in me: and the life which I now live in the flesh I live by the faith of the Son of God, who loved me, and gave himself for me." (Matthew 16:24; Galatians 2:20).

THE TREE AND RIVER OF LIFE

"In the midst of the street of it, and on either side of the river, was there the tree of life, which bare twelve manner of fruits, and yielded her fruit every month: and the leaves of the tree were for the healing of the nations" (Revelation 22:2).

The Tree of Life is described as singular, while at the same time it is "on either side of the river." This extraordinary tree, from which all the redeemed are free to eat, apparently has trunks on opposite banks of the river, and then above this river they merge into one enormous tree.

The Bible says that the tree bears "twelve manner of fruits, and yielded her fruit every month." Are all twelve kinds of fruit growing at once, or does a different crop of fruit appear on each of the twelve months? When we get to the New Jerusalem we can find out for ourselves.

When Adam and Eve fell into disobedience, they were banned from eating the fruit of this tree, for it possessed something by the grace of God that could perpetuate life. As mentioned above, the Lord placed "Cherubims" (angels), and a flaming sword to guard the way to the tree. This was done to prevent the pair from being able to "take also of the tree of life, and eat, and live for ever" (Genesis 3:22). Not only will we be given new, perfect bodies at the Second Coming of our Lord, but eternal youth will be ours, with free access to this amazing tree. Never again will anyone get sick, and there will be no more physical impairments for any of God's children.

"Then the eyes of the blind shall be opened, and the ears of the deaf shall be unstopped. Then shall the lame man leap as an hart, and the tongue of the dumb sing," "neither shall there be any more pain," "and the inhabitant shall not say, I am sick," "they shall run, and not be weary; and they shall walk, and not faint" (Isaiah 35:5,6; Revelation 21:4; Isaiah 33:24; 40:31).

Those who have been confined to a wheelchair will run like a deer. The formerly blind will have perfect vision. Those who have battled with cancer will forever have victory over their destructive foe. And bodies which have been deteriorated by old age will be granted eternal youth. Millions of people spend billions of dollars annually on products to make them look younger. Yet, ironically, the one source of never-ending youth and beauty is a free gift, available to all who will by living faith grab hold of it. Oh, to taste of the invigorating fruit of that tree! This is God's plan for you.

But what river is this over which the tree grows? "And he shewed me a pure river of water of life, clear as crystal, proceeding out of the throne of God and of the Lamb" (Revelation 22:1). The River of Life is this river, and it flows from the very throne of God Himself! God's creative power then, is constantly at work, supplying all of the inhabitants of this city with pure, refreshing water, "clear as crystal."

Those who drink from this literal river of life will have already tasted the refreshing spiritual waters that Christ has always offered. "Jesus stood and cried, saying, If any man thirst, let him come unto me, and drink" (John 7:37).

Jesus longs to give us the living water now so that the promise of the literal water can be fulfilled: "For the Lamb which is in the midst of the throne shall feed them, and shall lead them unto living fountains of waters" (Revelation 7:17). To taste of that river and be filled with the eternal youth and vitality it provides, is an experience not to be missed. "I will give unto him that is athirst of the fountain of the water of life freely," "And whosoever will, let him take the water of life freely" (Revelation 21:6; 22:17).

THE SEA OF GLASS

"And before the throne there was a sea of glass like unto crystal," "And I saw as it were a sea of glass mingled with fire" (Revelation 4:6; 15:2).

The sea of glass is as clear as crystal. Not only this, but it is either covered with fire or it reflects the glory from the throne of God so faithfully that it appears to have fire flashing and blazing across its surface. We get a limited picture of this sometimes near sundown on an ocean or lake; the sun reflecting off the water is almost blinding as it sparkles like millions of diamonds. This, however is utter darkness compared to the Sea of Glass.

When Christ was on this earth, He actually walked upon the water. Peter, by trusting in the power of the Savior was able to do so as well (see Matthew 14:25-31). But alas, as he took his eyes off Jesus and focused on the "boisterous" wind, in its manifestation through the waves, he was afraid, and his faith temporarily slipped. The moment his faith faltered, he started to sink, and cried out for the Lord to save him.

The Bible describes a people who will "stand on the sea of glass, having the harps of God" (Revelation 15:2). These redeemed ones, like Peter, are able to actually walk on the surface of this water. Their faith in Jesus will never slip. The very fact that this sea holds them up with every step will forever bear witness to their faith in the power of the Lamb.

ROBES AND PALMS

The Bible tells us that the faithful children of God will be given emblems of their victory through the blood of the Lamb. The prophet John describes them thus:

"After this I beheld, and, lo, a great multitude, which no man could number, of all nations, and kindreds, and people, and tongues, stood before the Lamb, clothed with white robes, and palms in their hands; And cried with a loud voice, saying, Salvation to our God which sitteth upon the throne, and unto the Lamb" (Revelation 7:9,10).

These white robes will be made of something we have never seen or felt before. The essence of light itself will clothe us as the glory from the throne of God shines upon us. When Moses asked the Lord "I beseech thee, shew me thy glory" (Exodus 33:18), God answered his request and passed before him, proclaiming His holy character. This was the incident in which God re-wrote the Ten Commandments on the tables of stone with His own finger (see Deuteronomy 10:1-4). As Moses came down from the mountain, after meeting and communing with God, his face shone so brightly that it frightened the people (see Exodus 34). This is what happens when beings dwell in the very presence of the Holy One. Of the redeemed it is prophesied: "And they shall see his face" (Revelation 22:4). Those who have "washed their robes, and made them white in the blood of the Lamb" have allowed the "filthy rags" of their own righteousness to be replaced by the perfect righteousness of Jesus Christ. Their sins they have allowed to be washed as clean and "white as snow" (Revelation 7:14; Isaiah 64:6; 1:18). Thus for all eternity their very robes—our robes—will testify to the amazing mercy of Jesus in covering us with His righteousness and paying the penalty that should have fallen on us. Throughout the ceaseless ages, not one of our sins will be mentioned to us, for they will all be forgotten (see Ezekiel 18:22, Hebrews 10:17).

So why the palm branches? The palm branch has long been a symbol of victory. When Jesus fulfilled the prophecy of Zechariah 9:9—that the King would ride into Jerusalem on a young donkey—the people "took branches of palm trees, and went forth to meet him, and cried, Hosanna: Blessed is the King of Israel that cometh in the name of the Lord" (John 12:13).

Those who inherit eternal life are described as "them that had gotten victory," "he that overcometh," "able to stand against the wiles of the devil," "able to quench all the fiery darts of the wicked," "he that endureth to the end," and "more than conquerors through him that loved us" (Revelation 15:2; 21:7; Ephesians 6:11,16; Matthew 10:22; Romans 8:37). The heavenly palm branch they receive symbolizes not their own efforts at living the victorious life, but rather their complete understanding that only Jesus could give them the victory they were so utterly incapable of achieving on their own. No matter how weak, sinful, and erring, the Lord tells the penitent soul, "My strength is made perfect in weakness" (2 Corinthians 12:9). This message will be immortalized in the palm branches.

THOSE FAMOUS STREETS

"And the street of the city was pure gold, as it were transparent glass" (Revelation 21:21).

Most people have heard of the streets of gold, even if they have never picked up a Bible. But this text reveals that they are not only gold, but transparent gold. We don't know how thick they will be, but imagine what it will be like to walk around on enormous, shining, golden streets that you can see right through. They will no doubt be mirror-shiny too, and will probably reflect the images of the golden city above. In the very midst of the main street flows that river of life, and on either side of the river grows the tree of life. The city itself is made of this same transparent, shining gold (see Revelation 21:18).

The gold upon which the redeemed will walk, represents their faith which has been tried in the fire and refined by God. Jesus admonished those in Laodicea, "I counsel thee to buy of me gold tried in the fire, that thou mayest be rich" (Revelation 3:18). And Peter, under inspiration of the Holy Spirit, advises us, "Wherein ye greatly rejoice, though now for a season, if need be, ye are in heaviness through manifold temptations: That the trial of your faith, being much more precious than of gold that perisheth, though it be tried with fire, might be found unto praise and honour and glory at the appearing of Jesus Christ" (1 Peter 1:6,7).

"The fining pot is for silver, and the furnace for gold: but the Lord trieth the hearts" (Proverbs 17:3).

"And [I, God] will refine them as silver is refined, and will try them as gold is tried: they shall call on my name, and I will hear them" (Zechariah 13:9).

"But he knoweth the way that I take: when he hath tried me, I shall come forth as gold" (Job 23:10).

Often the people of God find themselves, as did Job, in trials and afflictions that test their faith severely. This testing only refines and strengthens them, if they hold on to their trust in the almighty God. Just as one cannot build muscles unless there is resistance and exercise, so faith, when it lies dormant cannot flourish and grow. With each passing trial we not only have increased faith, but we more fully reflect the image of Jesus to those around us. As the gold on the heavenly streets reflects the glory and light of Jesus in the New Jerusalem, so the children of God have been called to reflect Christ on this earth (see 2 Corinthians 3:18). God's Word tells us to consider our trials as a means of building up our patience and faith.

"My brethren, count it all joy when ye fall into divers temptations; Knowing this, that the trying of your faith worketh patience. But let patience have her perfect work, that ye may be perfect and entire, wanting nothing" (James 1:2-4).

The splendor and beauty of the New Jerusalem will not only fascinate the senses of those who will call this city home, but will stand as eternal reminders of the great Plan of Salvation. The light from the throne of God permeates every corner of this gigantic metropolis. His children will eternally bask in these rays which brighten their new, perfect home. This is the same light made available to you and I today, only then we will view it unhindered by the distances of space. Jesus said, "I am the light of the world: he that followeth me shall not walk in darkness, but shall have the light of life" (John 8:12).

The light which can shine upon our minds and hearts today—removing darkness, doubt and spiritual confusion as to what is truth—is none other than Jesus Himself. He invites us to come to Him just as we are, and let His light shine life into our souls. As He is the source of all light on earth today, so He will be the source of all light in the Holy City.

"And the city had no need of the sun, neither of the moon, to shine in it: for the glory of God did lighten it, and the Lamb is the light thereof. And the nations of them which are saved shall walk in the light of it," "And there shall be no more curse: but the throne of God and of the Lamb shall be in it; and his servants shall serve him: And they shall see his face; and his name shall be in their foreheads. And there shall be no night there; and they need no candle, neither light of the sun; for the Lord God giveth them light" (Revelation 21:23,24; 22:3-5).

❖ ❖ ❖

The cloud which carries the Savior, all His angels, and now the redeemed, approaches heaven. What will this place be like, you wonder, as you peer ahead toward the growing light. Heaven! You have thought and dreamed about it for years on the earth, and now you will actually be seeing it! It's so hard to believe that this is all real! And yet it is. The moment that you have been waiting for all your life is now transpiring all around you.

The cloud begins its descent upon the Sea of Glass, which stretches out for miles before the Holy City. You immediately understand why the prophet John said it was mingled with fire. The light and the radiant gold from the city bounce off the surface of the crystal water so brightly it looks as though it really is on fire—perhaps it is!

You find yourself and the multitude around you lowered toward its gleaming surface and you are quickly engulfed by the light. The golden beams flicker all around you, and it is unlike anything you have ever experienced. It's hard to say whether this is fire or light, but it is a heavenly sight, and it surrounds you completely, whatever it is.

As your feet touch down, it feels soft and cool to your toes. If it is real fire, it surely isn't burning you. You take a step forward. The substance below you feels something like water, yet it supports you. Looking off to the horizon you notice that not a ripple or wave appears on its surface. It is indeed as smooth as glass, and clear as crystal below the light.

Jesus, head and shoulders above all others, stands in the middle of this glassy sea, surrounded by the innumerable new residents, who again behold His countenance. The magnificent wall of the city behind, although larger in size, is itself eclipsed by the beauty, glory, and brightness of the Savior. Human and angel bow before Him in love and adoration. Although He is the Son, He is fully God, deserving of worship. As you rise, you notice He is looking to the top of the city where the Father upon His throne overlooks the scene. All eyes follow the Redeemer's and ultimately land on the glorious light that envelops the Father Himself. You long to get a closer view; your wish will soon be granted.

Now Jesus leads the great multitude forward to enter into the City. Although you are surrounded by people and angels on every side, there is no sense of claustrophobia that often struck you in massive crowds on earth. The text "God is not the author of confusion, but of peace" (1 Corinthians 14:33), comes back to you as you and the vast company move forward, peacefully and in order, following the Savior.

Jesus, with His own mighty arm, lays hold of one of the pearly gates, and swings it back on its glittering hinges. Then the King who prepared this wonderful place for His children leads the great host through the giant portal. It occurs to you that the "narrow road" on earth ironically led you to the wide and accommodating gate of this place.

The massive wall is as gorgeous from its insides as it was from without. Everyone seems to be looking up as you walk through 216 feet of pure, heavenly jasper. You wonder how the rest of the city could possibly be more glorious than this grand tunnel through the wall. Looking ahead you see that some of the people have exited the tunnel, and they seem to be overwhelmed with delight and amazement as the even brighter light washes over them. Your loved one, still close by from the Resurrection, taps your shoulder and points up to a particularly beautiful portion of the overhead stone. You had forgotten she was beside you, having been so caught up in the wonder of it all.

Now you step out into the brilliance of the Holy City. What a sight for human eyes! This place is so vast, and there are so many new things to see! Grand fountains of water spray their giant arcs into the air. Lofty waterfalls, designed and constructed by the Redeemer Himself, cascade down the shimmering gold walls of some of the structures. Are these waterfalls actually branches of the River of Life, from the throne of the Almighty? Music from a million trumpets and stringed instruments fills the city as you wander from sight to sight. Such grand and powerful music it is, and yet it lacks that throb of discord so often blasted from the instruments of earth. The moving composition seems to fit perfectly with this majestic, yet peaceful kingdom.

Your attention is drawn to the very street upon which you stand. You knew it would be transparent gold, but your preconceived image of the substance didn't even come close. You cannot, as you gaze upon it, bring to mind any material that can rival its splendor. Beneath this street, and on either side of it, you notice the foundation of jasper. Its brilliant green reflection surpasses that of the wall, for you are now nearer the throne of God, which inundates the city with light.

This thought causes you to look up toward the throne, and as your eyes once again behold the Father on His Royal Chair, you marvel at the design and ingenious thought behind this city. Although the Great White Throne is 12 floors up, you can see it perfectly from this floor. In fact, you notice that the city has been designed, at least from your initial observations, so that the glory of God can be seen from any angle and any room in this gigantic, intricate city. Openings appear throughout the 12 foundations, and the foundations themselves are transparent. Never in this perfect city will you be without access to a clear view of the Father and the Lamb.

Trees of all sorts fill the city. One long stretch of fountains is lined by hundreds of towering palm trees. You look elsewhere and see the gorgeous willow tree, the lovely dogwood, the mighty oak. Sycamores decorate one street, while bright red and orange maples adorn another.

The golden structures within this place rise up to heights that dwarf the tallest earthly skyscrapers. How pitiful and skinny, frail and dull, were the grandest designs man had constructed. How temporary their existence in contrast to the perpetuity of what you now behold. Resplendent staircases of every height, shape and design ascend throughout the city and you wonder which to explore first. The thought recurs that you need not fret over how much you can do, for you have all of eternity in which to do it. Whatever area of this place remains unexplored within the first million years can be investigated within the next billion or so. Yet even then, as creative as the Lord is, you would still not have seen all that lies within the walls of this great metropolis. Truly there is no end to the handiwork of your Creator!

The multitude follows Jesus down the main street in the center of the city and up a giant staircase lined with massive, shining pillars. This staircase is enormous and its width appears to be several miles at least. All your life, you knew that this city would be big, but as you gaze upon it now, you begin to grasp just how gigantic it really is. On earth there was never a need for such a colossal staircase, but as the large company begins to ascend its glittering steps, you realize that there is function behind the form.

At the top of the staircase, Jesus leads this shining sea of people down a tremendous corridor. You are making your way toward the throne He shares with the Father, and every step seems to be more illumined as you close the distance. This corridor gives you a chance to look more closely at something you have seen on many of the buildings: It appears as though there are signs of some sort above the doors and you want to read one of them. A name which you do not recognize is carved in stone above the door frame. A soft voice tells you that it is the name of one of your fellow human beings. You turn and see the smiling face of an angel. He apparently had noticed your curiosity and wanted to answer your unspoken question. He then explains that soon you will be shown your own home which the Lord prepared just for you. The thought of a home right now, however, seems to pale in comparison to the One who made all this possible. The

Father and the Lamb, sitting on their throne, is an image which you have yearned to see up close and in person for so long, you can hardly believe it is about to be a reality.

After passing over several flights of stairs and exploring various parts of the city, you see that just up this last enormous staircase is the Great Throne Room. Something so bright it makes the sun appear as blackness, shines forth from the Origin of all life. Your anticipation is almost unbearable as you make your way up the stairs. The word "light" doesn't even seem to be adequate; this is something far more powerful than any light you've ever seen. Billions of angels are lifting their voices in praise as you finally reach the top of the staircase.

At the end of a long, golden aisle flanked by a myriad of angels presides God the Father. He sits atop the Royal Chair in all His glory and smiles at His Son who leads the redeemed to the foot of the Throne. You and the rest of the multitude bow low in the presence of the Sovereign of the universe. The Son of Man beholds with the Father the travail of His soul and is satisfied. All the beings in the city cry out, "Holy, Holy, Holy, is Him that sits upon the throne!" How long has the Father waited for this moment! How long has the Son yearned to witness this scene! The family of God, yea the "entire family named under heaven and earth" is finally together at last, never again to be parted. The work which Jesus did on behalf of the fallen race has yielded its precious fruit. The Holy Trinity—Father, Son, and Holy Spirit—have accomplished what they set out to do. Christ's image has been restored in the fallen race and love alone will reign throughout eternity. The Word of God expressed it best in three simple words: "God is love."

"For he shall give his angels charge over thee, to keep thee in all thy ways." —Psalm 91:11

"Are they not all ministering spirits, sent forth to minister for them who shall be heirs of salvation?" —Hebrews 1:14

The Bible makes it very clear that we each have a guardian angel. In fact, in times of danger or special need, we can be assured of the presence of multiple angels. Scripture tells us of an instance when the King of Syria decided to send an army on horseback to go and get the prophet Elisha. Elisha's servant saw the great host of soldiers and asked his master what they should do. Elisha's answer of faith is an assurance to us all: "Fear not: for they that be with us are more than they that be with them" (2 Kings 6:16). Then the prophet prayed that the Lord would open the eyes of his fearful servant, who immediately beheld that "the mountain was full of horses and chariots of fire round about Elisha" (verse 17).

Has our heavenly Father changed over the years? Is He less likely today to send an army of angels to protect us in time of need? "I am the Lord, I change not," is the promise from God Himself (Malachi 3:6). If the faith that humans exercise toward God has diminished over the centuries, it has not changed the fact that the angels are just as available today as they were in Bible times.

Imagine how thrilling it will be to finally meet that angel who has been guarding you all of your life. What a wonderful friendship is in store for you.

❖ ❖ ❖

You have only been in the Holy City a short time and your senses are overwhelmed by all of the sights and sounds. Glorious is the only word that comes to mind, but how short do words fall when describing this place. Your attention is turned once again to the tall, handsome, friendly-looking being that shines brightly beside you. This is the angel that joined you on your way up to meet the Lord in the air at the Second Coming. It is your guardian angel, and he is eager to talk with you! He tells you his name and you start to tell him yours, but then smile as you remember that this special friend has been by your side since the day you were born. He knew your name before you did. Since coming to this place, you also have a "new name" (Revelation 2:17). Unlike your old name, no one else in the entire universe has this name. It was chosen just for you by Jesus Himself.

The two of you stroll down the streets of gold amidst the celebration of the Great Homecoming. The rest of the redeemed are also meeting their angels for the first time, and all of the city seems to bustle with music, joyful reunions, angel activity, and people on the move.

As would be expected, you start to feel like you have known this angel all of your life. His smile radiates with the love of Jesus as he begins to tell you of the most fascinating incidents during his watch care over you.

All during your life on earth you had things that seemed to go wrong which you were determined to ask about when you got to heaven. But now the glory, peace, and joy that engulf your soul cause you to have trouble bringing those issues to mind. How petty the trials you had to endure when compared to this place! How temporary the struggles when contrasted with the eternity that lies before you! How insignificant the times of loneliness when compared to the fellowship with Jesus that you will enjoy as often as you wish! And now to think that through it all this angel was beside you, hurting when you hurt, watching over you in danger, and living for your well being!

Although you cannot bring any trials or disappointments to mind, your angel does relay some things to you that definitely shed some light on just such times. He mentions a few instances where you seemed sure that God did not hear your prayers. Then by the gift of prophecy he unfolds to you what would have happened had your prayer been answered the way you desired. He reveals the ultimate loss, whether temporal or eternal, that would have resulted from having things your way. Your appreciation of God only multiplies as you realize now more than ever that His ways are, without even the slightest exception, for our own good. All things do indeed work together for good to them that love Him (Romans 8:28).

Next your angel reveals to you a number of times that your life was saved and you weren't even aware of it; that flat tire you had, which caused you to cross a certain intersection 23 minutes later, thus avoiding the drunk driver; that 747 whose mechanical problems were delayed while you calmly read a magazine in seat 17C, oblivious to it all; that snake whose mouth was held shut as you stepped ignorantly over him during a summer stroll through the woods. You see more and more how the hand of the Lord through His angels, was keeping you safe at every moment.

And even when your body was allowed to be injured, as in the case of Job, you see that it was still God's loving, miraculous power that kept your heart beating and sustained you through it all.

You reach a giant, golden staircase that stretches up toward the colossal architecture overhead. You and your angel continue your conversation as you begin your ascent. God surely knew what He was doing when He assigned this angel to you. Your personalities seem to have something in common that goes beyond explanation. This will truly be one of your closest friends through all the ages. It is a friendship that will only grow as eternity marches on.

"Let not your heart be troubled: ye believe in God, believe also in me. In my Father's house are many mansions: if it were not so, I would have told you. I go to prepare a place for you. And if I go and prepare a place for you, I will come again, and receive you unto myself; that where I am, there ye may be also."

—John 14:1-3

Jesus has prepared a place for you. He has built you a home that you'll enjoy more than if you had designed it yourself. He knows what appeals to you more than you yourself know. As Creator of your particular personality, He knows exactly what design and style of home best suits your every need and want.

There is no doubt there will be mansions in heaven. When we consider who the Architect of that city is and when we read about it in Revelation 21 and 22, we know that there will be no shacks in the kingdom of God. In fact, the largest and most comfortable, luxurious homes on this old earth will pale in comparison. When we look at the actual Greek word for "mansions" in this text, *mone*, we see that it also means "a staying, or residence; abode." Now, the promise is that in Jesus' Father's *house* are many of these residences, which implies that the New Jerusalem, with its walls that stretch to the top of the city, is actually much like a colossal house, complete with mansions all interconnected in one giant mass of rooms.

In other words, although in size, shape, and material, these dwellings can only be described as "mansions," God our Father has designed the city so that His entire family, all of His children, will have a place in His enormous house, the New Jerusalem.

Unlike our future country homes, which will be surrounded by wide expanses of nature as far as the eye can see, these city homes will be a place where God's children can dwell among and in close fellowship with their brothers and sisters. Like any loving parent, God wants a place where all of His children can get together: sort of like the world's largest family reunion. Reader,

He wants you there as well. He invites you to be a part of the "whole family in heaven and earth," who are named after Christ Jesus (Ephesians 3:14,15), and to finally abide in your special place in His house.

❖ ❖ ❖

Your guardian angel has been showing you around the golden City. As you tour the place you are amazed at God's inexhaustible imagination and His boundless love for fallen humanity. Every object in sight seems to point to the glory of God; every gift is a reminder of the ultimate Gift in the life of the Son. Of all subjects to study, the one that you are most eager to investigate is Calvary's great Sacrifice on your behalf. And yet somehow you realize that even an eternity is not long enough to comprehend all of the love and self-humiliation involved in redeeming your soul and the souls of your brothers and sisters in Christ.

The great network of glorious buildings spreading out before you reveals ingenious design as well as beauty. The city is so breathtaking, only the glory of the Trinity Itself surpasses its splendor. Each floor in this grand design possesses its own unique style. Your hardest task is found in deciding which part you like the best. Regal staircases ascend into the lofty heights, gorgeous balconies decorate many of the mansions, radiant bridges span multiple buildings, and streets of gold criss-cross though the labyrinth of structures. The entire place is alive with movement as angel and human mingle along the walkways and bridges. Some of them wave from windows and balconies, as you pass below. You wave back and the thought comes to you that as eternity rolls on, you will get to know more and more of these people and angels, until every home and every street will be filled with "old friends." This thought makes exploring the place even more exciting.

Suddenly your eyes fall upon a house that stops you in your tracks. This home is no larger than any of the previous places you've seen, nor does it shine any brighter. But something about the way it's laid out just seems to hold your attention. Your angel tells you that you are more than welcome to take a closer look if you desire, and you nod without a word as the two of you head toward it.

This edifice is several stories high, although still within its particular foundation of the great twelve. The street in front of this home is bustling with life as people and angels pass to and fro, exploring houses and buildings all along this part of the city. Something about the way the various balconies are designed intrigues you. The multiple pillars in front tie into the roof in a way that curiously appeals to you. The windows are large and just the style you like. The front doors seem to say "come on in."

The angel then tells you what you already knew: this place is yours, designed and created just for you. A sense of your great unworthiness and Christ's remarkable affection for you fills your soul. The angel then offers to give you a tour. You eagerly agree, as your curiosity builds.

You cross the busy street and begin to ascend the massive staircase with the angel. Halfway up the stairs you get your first peek at who you assume must be your next door neighbor. He too is exploring his new home, and he waves from his balcony as soon as he sees you. You smile as you and your angel return the gesture. There is no need for words. You know by his expression that he is thinking the same thing you are: *I can't believe we're actually here!* You wonder when he lived upon the earth. It could have been during your life, but perhaps he lived during Jesus' day, or maybe Abraham's. You intend to find out very soon.

Above the large double doors you see your new name. Yes, Jesus did indeed go to prepare a place for *you.* And now you see it with your own eyes. Your greatest desire as you look at these doors is that He Himself should walk through them and grace this home with His presence as often as possible.

To enter the home you have no need for a key, for there are no locks in this land. All chances of burglary or any such crime have been forever left in the past. Your angel proceeds to lead you through the spacious house. Everything is perfect, and for once that word is not just a figure of speech. Not one square inch of this place should be changed. The Lord knew exactly what He was doing; He always has.

You wonder why there are so many large areas in this house, and the angel explains that it will be quite common for groups to get together and talk about heavenly things. These grand rooms allow for such gatherings. No one will be unable to invite large numbers of friends over due to a lack of space in the home, for all homes here are designed with just such a purpose in mind.

Other rooms are not so large, and seem almost quaint, even cozy. Every room has its purpose, and each is beautiful in its own unique way. On an upper floor, you enter your main dwelling room. Your new body has no need of sleep, but you still have a special room in which to go and have some quiet time if you wish. This room has a gorgeous view of the city for miles to the west, and as you step out onto the balcony, the city appears more beautiful from this angle than from anywhere else! Not only did God know what type of house matched you perfectly, but He also knew the exact view that would have the most pleasant effect on you. What a God is this, that you serve! The math involved in arranging all the homes so that the view is perfectly suited for each individual from their particular angle—while retaining that perfection for every other individual—is incalculable.

You rest your elbows against the edge of the balcony and shake your head in amazement. Suddenly you see a close friend walking with her angel down below and you call out her name. She looks up and smiles, then asks if that's your place. You tell her it is, and she tells you where her home is, so that you can stop by in the near future. She then continues on through the city as her angel points out all of the magnificent buildings along the way. You turn and sit down on a large, comfortable chair beside the angel. Taking a deep breath of the pure, fresh city air, you lean back in your seat. Your angel and you remain silent for a moment as you take in the fabulous vista. The glittering of the city's horizon once again brings your thoughts to God. How well He knows you. How much He loves you. At last you have found a home, a place to forever call your own. In your Father's house there really are many rooms for His children. This one was made just for you.

REVERSAL OF FORTUNE

"Blessed are they that mourn: for they shall be comforted."
—Matthew 5:4

The news is almost unbearable to watch these days. Reading the newspaper eliminates the visual impact of TV news, but the pain so often detailed in black ink still drives the point home: this is not a world of happiness. Children are being abused. Wives are being beaten. Young people are being told they are worthless. Mothers are killing their own babies. Kids are shooting each other. Wars and natural disasters are snuffing out the lives of thousands, and health problems shorten or ruin the lives of millions.

And yet we see only the tip of the iceberg. Imagine how the Lord must feel; He sees it all. Not one person's feelings are crushed without Him taking notice. Not one child is slapped without Him seeing. Not one wife is beaten out of His eyesight. All of the suffering in this world, experienced by every human from the greatest to the weakest, He sees and records. But more than that, He feels. It hurts Jesus actually more than it hurts the one in pain. Who would you rather have suffer, a loved one or yourself? It is the same with God. He cannot bear to witness all the pain and heartache that occur daily in this world. We would do well to remember that there is a limit to how far He will allow the suffering to continue. Soon He will return in the clouds of glory to "give every man according as his work shall be" (Revelation 22:12).

On that day all suffering will end. Those who languish in pain and misery now, who are abused and mistreated at the hands of others, will very soon have a reversal of fortune.

Are you one such person, reader? Maybe your trials are not in the area of physical abuse or faltering health, but rather mental abuse or hatefulness. Or perhaps your trials have nothing to do with people intentionally mistreating you, but you are just going through a particularly rough time right now: your job situation, your money problems, your addictions, your wayward loved ones. Whether physical or mental, trial or temptation, our Lord pronounces a special blessing upon you if you are somehow suffering. He says that though you may mourn now, if you give yourself over to Him, you will indeed be comforted. And He assures you that "your sorrow shall be turned into joy" (John 16:20). The comfort He promises, you can claim right now, in this old world. Always remember that the same Jesus who desires to walk with you beside the river of life, is walking beside you today, though you may not always sense it. Christ declared that He came to this world so that you might have a more abundant life (see John 10:10). The Christian is able to have strength through the trials, for he or she possesses something that non-believers utterly lack: a Rock upon whom to place their burdens, a Shepherd who tenderly watches His sheep, an Intercessor to forgive their sins.

In fact, one of the names given to the Holy Spirit by Christ Himself is "the Comforter" (John 16:7). If we can grasp this thought, then when trials come—no matter how severe or apparently permanent—we can be comforted by the fact that God is still in charge and will soon put an end to all injustice.

"Beloved, think it not strange concerning the fiery trial which is to try you, as though some strange thing happened unto you: But rejoice, inasmuch as ye are partakers of Christ's sufferings: that, when his glory shall be revealed, ye may be glad also with exceeding joy" (1 Peter 4:12,13).

❖ ❖ ❖

You have been in the New Jerusalem for but a short time. Your guardian angel is taking you on a personal tour of the glorious place and now he says he has a few people he would like to show you. You follow him, eager to see what he has in mind.

The city is so immense that even inside its walls appear fields of green grass and acres of giant trees. A group of people dressed in shining white gather beneath the boughs of one such tree.

Close by, several little ones help each other scale the back of a grand lion, who sits patiently among them.

Your angel points out one of the children: a little boy you estimate to be about 8 years old. He explains that this child was abused for most of his short life. The drunken father had made a habit of slapping the child around for every little thing. Even if something got broken by accident, and even if it was not this child's fault, "daddy" would inflict wounds on the boy that would take days, sometimes weeks, to heal.

Now the child's face just glows with happiness. In the old earth, several of his little teeth had been knocked out. But here his playful smile reveals a complete set of pearly-whites. He laughs with glee as he finally mounts the majestic creature, and strokes its gorgeous mane.

You step back onto main street, its transparent gold surface sparkling under your feet. A little farther down the busy street the angel points out a lovely woman robed in white, smiling as she talks with her former guardian. He explains that this beautiful woman was nearly devoid of any self worth in the old world. At times she had been teased for her extremely homely face, which had been disfigured in a car accident when she was only a toddler. She had no real friends all through grade school or high school and the college years had proven only slightly better. Often she had contemplated suicide and felt that no one would notice her departure. But just after college someone had befriended her and treated her like a real person of value. That someone ultimately led her to Christ, who finally gave her peace and a knowledge of her true worth. She discovered that when the King of the universe comes all the way down to earth and dies for your sake, you must not be such a worthless person after all.

As you are speaking, two boys and a girl run by at an incredible speed, laughing as they go. Your angel tells you that these three had been paralyzed, and that they now excel in speed. For all eternity their strong legs will be a testimony to the power and love of God.

Your eyes follow them as they run past a great, marble table loaded with food. At this table sits a large group of people. Your angel reveals that these are just a fraction of those Christians who had died of starvation in the third world countries of the old earth. The bodies of these people are now filled with strength and energy, and it's obvious that a lack of food will never again be a problem.

Up ahead and to the right of the street you see what looks like a giant park. Thousands upon thousands of people and angels are gathered here, and soon you see why. At the northern end of the park, a gentle hill rises from the plain. Jesus sits upon this hill and in his lap are several little children. The crowd listens eagerly as He reveals some of the things He has planned for them. He must have just recently come to this park, for as the people become aware of His location, they quickly descend on the place. The crowd is growing by the minute.

Your angel points out a little girl sitting on the knee of the Savior. What better place in all the universe to be? What safer place is there in all creation? The angel informs you that this girl's family had been taken captive during one of the old earth wars and she had witnessed the torture and death of her father. The barbaric and inhumane treatment that she and her mother were subjected to for months on end was worse than death itself. Incomparably evil were the deeds that men could do when the passion of war burned through their veins.

But now this little innocent child sits on the lap of the Lord, her mother and father reclining beside Him. Smiles rest on every face in this new land, and all have forgotten the trials of days gone by. The cursed lot that so many had to bear and the fortune of countless suffering souls has for all eternity been reversed.

"And God shall wipe away all tears from their eyes; and there shall be no more death, neither sorrow, nor crying, neither shall their be any more pain: for the former things are passed away" (Revelation 21:4).

"And the former shall not be remembered, nor come into mind" (Isaiah 65:17).

"His lord said unto him, Well done, good and faithful servant; thou hast been faithful over a few things, I will make thee ruler over many things: enter thou into the joy of thy lord."

—Matthew 25:23

What exactly is the joy of our Lord? What is it we shall "enter into" when we get to heaven? The Bible gives us some clues.

"Looking unto Jesus, the author and finisher of our faith; who for the joy that was set before him endured the cross" (Hebrews 12:2).

According to the Bible, the joy of our Lord is found in saving lost souls. Jesus endured the Cross by contemplating the future joy brought about in the final redemption of our race. True joy for Him is found in beholding all of those who will gain eternal life through His work on their behalf.

Another thing that brings our Lord joy is seeing His children accept the Sacrifice provided for their sins, repenting of those sins, and turning away from them.

"Likewise I say unto you, there is joy in the presence of the angels of God over one sinner that repenteth" (Luke 15:10).

God and angels rejoice over one sinner that repents here on earth today—*one* sinner. They are not indifferent to the lives of individuals, neither are they waiting on a great reformation on earth to awaken their interest in us. No, we are told that even one person who comes to God in sincere confession and repentance of sin, can bring about joy in heaven.

"Now unto him that is able to keep you from falling, and to present you faultless before the presence of his glory with exceeding joy" (Jude 24).

Not only does the sinner's acceptance of His death on the Cross bring joy to our Lord, not only does the sinner's repentance bring Him joy, but we're told that His ability to give us victory over sin brings Him "exceeding joy." He loves us too much to forgive us and then leave us chained to the sins that so easily beset us. He wants to break those chains, to set the captives free, to abide in us so that we no longer do those soul-destroying things. It is in this victory which He works out through us, that He finds exceeding joy.

Thus, if we are to enter into His joy when He comes back to receive His servants, we should be entering into His joy here, while souls are perishing all around us.

"Let him know that he which converteth the sinner from the error of his way shall save a soul from death, and shall hide a multitude of sins" (James 5:20).

The Lord calls upon us to seek out His lost sheep. We are all God's children, and the only true way to enter into His joy, is to partake in His reaching out to the lost: those who know Him not. This act, done in the love of God, with all patience and without criticism or judging, will surely bear its fruit and bring us a joy that we will eternally share with our Lord. Jesus even prayed that "they might have *my joy* fulfilled in themselves" (John 17:13).

While Christ is to forever be the focus of all praise, honor, and glory, the redeemed will enjoy seeing the fruits of their labors. Many a soul will in that day approach the humble instrument that God used, and thank him or her for their guidance which led to the foot of the Cross. Many a child will gladly proclaim of his mother and/or father, "It is because of their efforts, their loving guidance, their Christ-centered priorities in my upbringing, that I am here today."

In other cases it is the parents who embrace the child in gratitude for the perseverance which they demonstrated by the grace of God. Friends, co-workers, relatives, and acquaintances will not be forgetful of the person or people so influential in their lives. Some people will for the first time be made aware of the prayers which had been ascending to heaven on their behalf from a concerned loved one.

In heaven it will not even be considered what job we had in this life, or how many cars we owned; what degrees we attained from college or how many awards we received; how handsome or beautiful we were, or whether or not we achieved any worldly fame. The only question that will matter as far as our course of action is concerned, is whether or not we advanced the cause of God. Did we reach out to uplift our fellow human beings? Were we fully submitted to the will of our Father in heaven? Did we, by our words and lives, reveal the crucified Savior to a dying world around us? Only on that day will we truly get a clear view of the bigger picture. Only then will we realize just how much the Holy Spirit influenced others by the way we lived our lives. And only then will we truly share in the fullness of our Lord's joy.

"And they that be wise shall shine as the brightness of the firmament; and they that turn many to righteousness as the stars for ever and ever" (Daniel 12:3).

❖ ❖ ❖

You are on your way to the great Marriage Supper with several dear friends and loved ones when suddenly you spot the person who brought you to Christ. She is also walking toward the grand table and then she looks your way. Your eyes meet, and her face lights up as she recognizes you. Immediately she runs over and embraces you. This is not out of character for her, as loving kindness was a normal part of her personality, even in the old earth. Love and appreciation flow freely from your lips as you both proclaim the boundless mercy and grace of God. No shred of pride emanates from your friend about how she brought you to the Lord—just humble praise to the One from whom comes all power. This is, and was, a person quite aware of the fact that without Jesus we can do nothing. You know this to be true, for had she been trying to influence you with her own abilities, there would have been no appeal to her testimony.

You both keep repeating that you can't believe you're actually here, and you quickly plan a time when you can get together and just sit back and talk. Suddenly there's a tap on your shoulder, and you turn to see a beautiful woman, just radiant with joy. You don't recognize her, and then she begins to explain that the last time you saw her she was in her nineties, and you had kindly volunteered to come over and work around her house for her. While there, you had given her a small book which showed her how to have a relationship with Jesus. That little act planted the seed which led to her acceptance of Christ. You had no idea what the results would be, but you had given it to her and prayed about it, trusting in God to do His part. That was the last time you had ever seen this elderly woman, until right now. What a change has taken place! Such a beautiful young lady stands before you in her luminous white robe; it's hard to believe this is the same person. She gives you a hug and acts as though she doesn't want to let go. You both praise Jesus, knowing that He is the tie that will bind your friendship forever and ever.

You loosen your embrace and she starts to walk with your group toward the giant Marriage Supper table. As you make your way down the golden street, you spot another friend from the old earth. Him you recognize, for you had been quite close. He and a another man hurry over to you and he also gives you a hefty bear hug. You quickly introduce him to your new friend, and he begins to explain to her how you brought him to Christ as well. He tells her that at first he was taken back by you talking about Jesus so much. He thought you were a bit too strait-laced. But eventually your cheerful disposition was far too contagious for him, and he had to find out more about who Jesus *really* was. Your secret prayers had also affected his heart although he didn't find out about those prayers until months later.

His friend now begins to explain how he had led *him* to Christ. His story underscores the fact that each person who is brought into the kingdom brings others in as well. By the grace of God, this cycle had been continuously repeated throughout earth's history. The value of even one soul is more apparent than ever as you realize the multiplication factor involved. Not only did you directly influence all of those you introduced to Jesus, but you indirectly influenced all of the ones they influenced, and all of the people *they* influenced: and so on, and so on.

As you walk along, talking with your friends, you see in the distance among a band of angels a woman whose harsh attitude toward you had been met with kindness in return. Her presence here is the fruit of that kindness, which led her to Christ. Over there by one of the grand fountains walks that formerly homeless man whom you fed and to whom you spoke of Jesus' love. He went on to study the Bible with you and ultimately got his life back on track.

By the Tree of Life stands a woman who had been enslaved by a horrible addiction, but who found no freedom in the message of her counselors. She had been lulled to sleep by the belief that this addiction was just a part of who she was, and that she should never expect to gain the victory. The Holy Spirit had prompted you to go and speak from the Scriptures the words of encouragement that yes, indeed, Jesus is able to "proclaim liberty to the captives" and to "keep you from falling." By faith, her life had been transformed.

And over by the banks of the River of Life stands that former religious hypocrite. He had been judgmental in his criticism of others, which caused many to avoid his presence. But you and another friend sought him out and invited him to your weekly small study group. He saw in your group something that he knew had been missing in his life, and you showed him that that "something" was Jesus.

In your life on the earth you had not been able to hold the love of God inside. You were so liberated by it, and joyful in it, that you just could not keep quiet. This love didn't come from you naturally, but was a supernatural gift from God. What a privilege it was to promote the cause of God! And how thankful you will always be that while there was still time to make a difference, that privilege had been given to you. Only now do you fully comprehend the true joy of the kingdom of God. It's not merely in experiencing all of the wonderful things God has prepared for you; it is found in both fellowship with your Creator, and seeing with your own eyes, the happiness experienced by those for whom you prayed, worked, and cared. This was the will of God for His children. Of such is the kingdom of heaven.

"Blessed are they which are called unto the marriage supper of the Lamb." —Revelation 19:9

"The kingdom of heaven is like unto a certain king, which made a marriage for his son, and sent forth his servants to call them that were bidden to come to the wedding: and they would not come. Again he sent forth other servants, saying, Tell them which are bidden, Behold, I have prepared my dinner: my oxen and my fatlings are killed, and all things are made ready: come into the marriage. But they made light of it, and went their ways, one to his farm, another to his merchandise." —Matthew 22:2-5

Christ not only returned to heaven to prepare a place for you, but He also desires to have a wedding feast with you when you get there.

"He shall feed his flock like a shepherd," "And I say unto you, That many shall come from the east and west, and shall sit down with Abraham, and Isaac, and Jacob, in the kingdom of heaven," "That ye may eat and drink at my table in my kingdom" (Isaiah 40:11; Matthew 8:11; Luke 22:30).

Will this feast have real food? If we're going to go by the Bible, then the answer is most definitely, yes. Jesus declared, "But I say unto you, I will not drink henceforth of this fruit of the vine, until that day when I drink it new with you in my Father's kingdom" ("until the kingdom of God shall come") (Matthew 26:29; Luke 22:18). Jesus will drink the "fruit of the vine" with His followers in heaven, just as He drank it with them at the Last Supper. And after His resurrection, Jesus, in His glorified body, was given real food by the disciples. "And he took it, and did eat before them" (Luke 24:43). Our bodies will be like Christ's (see Philippians 3:21), and since His glorified body consumed food, ours will as well. "And they shall plant vineyards, and eat the fruit of them" (Isaiah 65:21).

The food at this supper will be like that enjoyed in the Garden of Eden. Before death entered into our world through sin, the food, like the rest of the planet, was perfect, for it had just come from the Creator's hand. The fruits and vegetables we eat today from the grocery store aren't nearly as tasty as vine- or tree-ripened food. And yet even the latter is nothing compared to the delicacies that await us in heaven! For thousands of years the foods we eat have been getting further and further away from their original taste that Adam and Eve enjoyed. In fact, in the last 100 years, the soil of the world's best farmlands has been so depleted of nutrients that the elder generation claims to even taste a difference.

What is your favorite fruit? Peaches? Blueberries? Watermelon? Bananas? Whatever it is, forget everything you know about it. The flavor there will make the sweetest, most succulent fruit here taste like sawdust. To many people, the idea of eating natural foods in heaven seems boring, because they have thrived on a diet of junk food for so long, their taste buds have been perverted. What they don't realize is that even their favorite high cholesterol, artery-packing, health-destroying food is by comparison bland and tasteless. Blueberry pie à la mode? Eating it in heaven would be sheer punishment due to lack of flavor. Deep-dish pizza with everything on it? The taste buds would hardly notice it. Hot cinnamon rolls with frosting oozing down the sides? Even this favorite pales in comparison to what is in store for you. We must continually grasp the thought that "Eye hath not seen, nor ear heard, [nor mouth tasted,] neither have entered into the heart of man, the things which God hath prepared for them that love him" (1 Corinthians 2:9).

This brings us to our next question: Do you love Him? The parable of the Marriage Supper describes many of those who were invited. It says of them, "they would not come," "they made light of it, and went their ways, one to his farm, and another to his merchandise" (Matthew 22:3,5).

Sharing the Marriage Supper with Christ is more than just sitting down to eat and drink the delicious foods of Paradise. It is accepting Him into our hearts today, and counting everything else in this world but loss. Notice that those who did not want to come to the feast went to their "farm" and "merchandise." The farm represents our work, our achievements, the things that occupy our time and minds. Are we putting these things above the Creator? If so, we are as truly making idols for ourselves as did the heathens of old. "Thou shalt have no other gods before me" is the first of the Ten Commandments (Exodus 20:3). No one comes to the Wedding Feast who does not put the King of the feast first in his or her life. The Lord forces Himself upon no one; it must be a willing decision.

The "merchandise" represents all of our material things we so often cherish above salvation itself. These too can become another god before Him who alone should sit upon the throne of our hearts. In the parable recorded in Luke we get even more excuses for missing out on the Great Supper. One had just bought some land that he put ahead of the feast. Another had just purchased five yoke of oxen that he felt he should put to good use right away. Still another had just gotten married, and had placed his spouse above his chance to attend the feast (See Luke 14:16-20).

Long is the list of reasons to be absent from the Marriage Supper which Jesus has so graciously planned for us. Many are the excuses for our delay in putting Christ first. To accept Jesus as our personal Savior and to abide in Him daily is the only chance we have to sit down with Him at the Great Feast.

In the Marriage Supper parable not only do we find people making excuses, but we actually discover one man who thought he could attend the feast without the wedding garment. The king who prepared the feast finds this man, and says to him, "Friend, how camest thou in hither not having a wedding garment?" (Matthew 22:12). The guest was "speechless," and was cast out of the feast into "outer darkness."

Without the wedding garment—the robe of Christ's righteousness—we will never sit down at that fabulous supper. Anything less than Christ's righteousness covering us represents our own attempts at righteousness which the Bible describes as "filthy rags" (Isaiah 64:6). At the same time, this robe that Christ offers will never cover chosen, ongoing sin, but rather is a reflection of the Holy Spirit dwelling in us. And the Holy Spirit in us causes us to walk in God's statutes and keep His judgments, so that we no longer walk after our favorite sins (See Ezekiel 36:26; Galatians 5:16; Acts 5:32).

"He that covereth his sins shall not prosper: but whoso confesseth and forsaketh them shall have mercy" (Proverbs 28:13).

"Blessed is he that watcheth, and keepeth his garments" (Revelation 16:15).

"To Him that overcometh will I give to eat of the hidden manna" (Revelation 2:17).

Jesus longs to sup with you at the Wedding Feast that is soon to take place. He's standing at the door of your heart. He's asking you to invite Him into your heart and give yourself completely to the One who will never let you down.

"Behold, I stand at the door, and knock: if any man hear my voice, and open the door, I will come in to him, and will sup with him, and he with me" (Revelation 3:20).

❖ ❖ ❖

You walk amidst the vast multitude that is following Jesus to the great Wedding Feast table. As Christ approaches the banquet He calls out for all of His precious souls to come join in the supper that He has prepared. Everyone shouts, "Alleluia! Glory!" as the procession continues to move forward and surround the giant table.

This table flashes with the most brilliant pure silver, and it appears to be many miles in length. As you approach the grand setting, you notice that a place has been prepared just for you. Your new name is written in the most beautiful style of handwriting and you wonder if the Savior Himself wrote it. You will ask Him about this later.

There is something exciting about being among such an enormous sea of people. This place is still very new to you and you haven't gotten used to seeing so many people in one place yet. The table shines exceptionally bright as all the redeemed press close to its reflective surface. The light from their robes seems to set the table ablaze in shimmering white.

As you sit at your place, you again contemplate the love of the Savior in making all of this possible. Not one thought of self-righteousness creeps into your mind. Such is the case with all of the saved. All praise and glory and honor go to the Lamb who was slain for your sins. The blessings He pours out on His children just seem to keep coming.

You lean forward and peer to your left. What a sight! A glorious table many miles in length, attended by all of these people! You look to your right: the view is equally impressive. It is astounding to think that every person in the history of the world who was ultimately cleansed by the blood of the Lamb is now sitting at this same place. Moses sits among this assembly. David can be found here. Joseph, Noah, Rachel, Paul—even Adam, the father of the entire race—all have their place at this very table.

Spread out before you is the most delightful food your eyes have ever beheld. There are the grapes, so giant and plump. The large figs are sure to be delicious. The almonds, pomegranates, peaches, cherries, dates, strawberries, and all the other fruits appear to be ready to burst their skins with their sweet fillings. And in a tall goblet you see the fruit of the vine that Christ was so fond of on the earth. Today He will drink it with all His faithful children, just as He promised. You can hardly wait for the feast to start; this will be your first taste of heavenly food.

Innumerable shouts of praise rise up from the table in gratitude to the Savior. Here there is no need to have prayer before eating, for all can thank Him in person. The shouts continue to rise as Jesus begins to visit His children at the massive table. He is fulfilling His promise to give the overcomers a share of the heavenly manna! He need not carry a giant basket, for just as He multiplied the bread on the earth for the "5,000" He can multiply it here for this multitude. Your heart seems to skip a beat as you see that He is now working His way near your part of the table!

Finally the King of kings reaches down onto your plate and places the most lovely, delicate, white piece of food you have ever seen. You are about to get your first taste of heavenly manna, and it looks delicious. But what really catches your eye is the nail print in the Savior's hand which holds the manna. What an image to behold. The One whose hands were pierced for you now stands beside you, serving you with that very same hand. You are not overcome by a shameful weight of guilt, for Jesus has taken care of all that. Rather, a sense of love and gratitude for this Man washes over you. He gave His very life so that you could be here with Him. The scarred hand now moves from the manna and rests on your shoulder. He knows your thoughts without your expressing them. You look up and your eyes meet the kindest face ever seen. You wish for nothing more than to spend an eternity with this Man, and it stirs your heart to know that it is exactly what He wants as well.

The Marriage Supper of the King is now a reality. The Wedding Feast is under way. All who heeded the merciful invitation are present for this grand event. Every guest is clothed with the wedding garment. As you taste the succulent food that covers this table and consider the hands that prepared it, you thank the Lord that you have not missed the wonderful occasion. The great Shepherd feeds His flock and gives them a taste of the heavenly manna. "Blessed are they which are called unto the marriage supper of the Lamb." Blessed shall they always be.

BEHOLD ALL THINGS NEW

"And he that sat upon the throne said, Behold, I make all things new." —Revelation 21:5

No human being has ever witnessed the creation of a planet. On the first day of our earth's history, God made light. On the second day He created our atmosphere. On the third day He made the land and called forth all plant life. On the fourth day He made the sun and moon, and the stars that are visible from this planet. On the fifth day God created all the marine life of the deep and the birds that cleave the air. But it wasn't until the sixth day—His last day of creating, and after all of the other creatures had been made—that human beings were formed. Thus, by the time Adam and Eve took their first breath, the entire planet was up and running. Their home, as it were, had been built before their arrival. The only thing they saw God make was the Sabbath day.

But this will not be the case when the earth is made new. Although Jesus has indeed returned to heaven to prepare a place for us, we are promised that one day this entire earth will be made new, and right before our eyes!

"And I saw a new heaven and a new earth: for the first heaven and the first earth were passed away" (Revelation 21:1).

The prophet John faithfully records what he saw in vision, and this is in harmony with the words of another prophet: "Nevertheless we, according to his promise, look for new heavens and a new earth, wherein dwelleth righteousness" (2 Peter 3:13; see also Isaiah 65:17; 66:22).

After the Holy City comes down to earth from heaven (Revelation 21:2) and the final judgment is executed (see *Strange Fire* chapter), then all of the redeemed will be able to watch the creative power of the Lord in action. "Behold," says the Lord, or, "Watch what is going to happen now." And then He says, "I make all things new." Nothing, nothing in this old world is worth missing out on that event. Jesus has the power to re-create this planet, but never forget this: it cannot be truly complete without you there. You are among those that Christ wants to place on the surface of that new earth. You are God's child, and when families get together, the parents desire nothing more than to have all the children present. Determine today that by the grace of God you will be there when the Father, Son, and Holy Spirit once again make all things new.

❖ ❖ ❖

You are standing atop the western wall of the New Jerusalem, peering down at the surface of the earth. The brilliant jasper shimmers under your feet. Suddenly you hear a voice, beautiful as many waters, yet mighty as thunder. "Behold," it rumbles, "I make all things new!"

You eagerly step closer to the edge of the wall beside three of your companions and all four guardian angels as the words roll across the face of the earth. The God you serve has the power to create with just a word, and He proceeds to tell the earth what to do.

"Let there be light!" He commands. Now the light that shines from the throne of He and the Lamb bursts out from the city and bathes the entire earth. There will never again be the need for a sun on this planet, for "the Lord God giveth them light" (Revelation 22:5).

You listen as God commands the lakes and rivers to appear. This time the earth is not to have the majority of its surface cloaked by the oceans, however (Revelation 21:1). These bodies of water are still enormous, but they don't rob humans of so much land as they did after the great Flood (Genesis 7:11). You watch as watery blue regions dot the various parts of the new earth.

Next the Lord commands that new trees and fresh plant life should appear. A beautiful carpet of green, spotted with trees of every variety, rolls out from the base of the city. It is an awesome sight. The creative energy involved seems to shake the very atmosphere and the sound is overpowering, yet not painful to the ears. To see a tree formed from nothingness is quite a thing to behold. These trees are perfect, and you look forward to tasting their fruit and climbing some of the larger ones. No doubt you will recline under a number of them during some of your many talks with Jesus.

Flowers decorate the land with their vivid colors. Some of the rolling hills are speckled with red, while others wear shades of blue. The level plains that stretch out for miles are also covered with a panoply of floral beauty. One field is loaded with bright white daisies and the bank of a tiny creek is lined with daffodils. Tulips and roses, lilies and carnations, all have their place in this gorgeous new world.

Again the mighty voice calls forth life, only this time they are lives on the move. Graceful birds now fill the air, and some in their spectacular flight formations seem to pay homage to their Creator. Others land in the freshly made trees and begin to sing and chirp in delight. Still others fly over the walls of the city and begin to explore that vast domain. One lands on your shoulder and playfully rubs its head against your neck. It appears to be a small hawk of some sort and you reach over to lift him onto your wrist. No fear resides within this bird. Unlike the wild fowls of old earth, these birds love the companionship of people. As you move him in front of your face, you start to ponder what you should name your new friend. You get distracted, however, as another, much larger bird soars directly over your head and into the city. Its wingspan must be 20 feet or more, and you try and recognize this species from the old earth. But before it lands, your attention is diverted again by that mighty voice you love so much.

The Creator commands that the land animals appear, and now the green of the earth below begins to stir with activity. Vast herds of buffalo come forth, the breath of life just bursting from their lungs. The landscape seems to erupt with life as the thundering sea of buffalo curves toward the south in spectacular formation. The sound of millions of hooves mingles with the thousands of other herds that are charging across the plains and hills.

Horses, antelope, elephants, zebras, sheep, deer, every beautiful and perfect creature that moves in numbers, comes forth to beautify the planet and fill it with motion. All of God's creatures are appearing. The bears, lions, kangaroos, wolves, rabbits, and squirrels, along with innumerable other creatures, materialize before your eyes and begin to enjoy their tailor-made habitat in perfect harmony.

Far below, you notice that the redeemed have started to exit the city and explore the wonders of God's handiwork. The angels grab the hands of you and your friends, and step over the edge of the wall for an exhilarating ride down to the surface. Your hawk friend quickly takes flight and follows your lead.

You see a group of bears playing beside a churning, white river in the distance and you anxiously head off toward them. As you do so, a giant herd of horses overtakes you and you find yourself surrounded by thousands of pounding hooves. You have no fear of any bodily harm and you stop to experience this thrill. Several of your friends are only a few feet away, and you look at each other in mutual amazement as the stampede rumbles by. Finally the last of the horses gallop past and as you watch them head toward the horizon, it occurs to you that later on you can ride any one of them that you wish. There are no fees to pay, no lessons required, and no chance of getting hurt.

Suddenly an enormous lion runs by, and he's followed by dozens more. They are chasing one another, and you decide to join them. You dash up the side of a hill and then down the other side, surrounded by the massive felines. Several of them roar as they head toward the giant valley below. You are amazed that you can actually keep up with them and you increase your speed as the incline steepens. At the bottom, a few of them playfully lunge at each other, like overgrown house cats. One turns and charges back up the hill, and you quickly try to catch him. At the top of the hill, you stop to scan this view of the new world as the lion circles you and then calmly plops down by your side.

The bears by the river once again attract your attention, and you start back down the hill to give them a visit. As you approach them, one lumbers over to greet you. She is smaller than the others and she licks your face playfully. Then the two of you race toward the river, where her fellow bears are gathered. Not one of them flees as you charge toward them. You are eternally sharers of a habitat, and nothing will ever ruin that.

The light from the throne of God and the Lamb gives everything a beautiful golden hue much like the last hour before sundown on old earth, only brighter and more glorious. You sit beside the river's edge and lean against a pine tree. As the hawk settles back onto your shoulder, a few new thoughts come to mind. The massive rocks that make up the riverbed will never, ever bear the selfish marks of graffiti. The tree you lean against will never be burned for pasture land. A thorn-free rose which you pick will never die. These massive herds that roam the prairies will never diminish in number. This water rushing in front of you will always be safe to drink. The air that you breathe will never contain a trace of pollution. All is in God's hands. The planet is safe forevermore; danger is eternally a thing of the past. What a wonderful place is this planet of yours. Behold, all things are new.

Inheritance of the Meek

"Blessed are the meek: for they shall inherit the earth."
—Matthew 5:5

"But the meek shall inherit the earth; and shall delight themselves in the abundance of peace." —Psalm 37:11

The earth, the land, is one of the most sought after, precious resources to the human race. More wars have been fought over land than anything else in history, and it was, in fact, a promised "land" that the Israelites sought during their 40 years in the wilderness.

At the very dawn of humanity, God put Adam and Eve in a garden so that they could "dress it and keep it" (Genesis 2:15). Humans were created to enjoy the land, and have done so ever since.

Just as in the case of your City home, the Lord knows more about the type of land that you would desire than you yourself do. When the earth is made new, He will lead you to the land that you have inherited by His merits. This landscape He will have designed with you particularly in mind.

When we think we really want something like a certain piece of property or a house or car, we find that after we have it, the excitement slowly fades. We begin to wonder why that particular thing was so important to us and soon we're infatuated with something else. Not so with the land you are to inherit. Never in a trillion years will you begin to grow tired of it. Never will you find another plot that suits your fancy better. The Lord will be giving you the land that fits your desires and personality better than any other land in the new earth (or the entire universe for that matter). Were you to pick your land, you would choose incorrectly. But your Father knows you better than you know yourself. After all, He created your tastes and desires, and He knows exactly what will make you the happiest. The greatest thing of all about the land you will inherit, and the house that you will build is the opportunity to invite Jesus over for a visit. If He is a welcome guest of yours now, He will be a regular guest of yours then.

❖ ❖ ❖

Christ and you are walking along a hillside covered with brilliant orange poppies. They wave in the breeze as their Creator walks by. Jesus puts His hand on your shoulder as you talk to each other. His touch feels so caring, and you have never been more at ease in your life. This man—this real man who walks beside you—actually came down to the old earth and allowed Himself to take your punishment. All of those sins that you committed He took upon Himself. By His stripes from the whip you were saved and healed. You wonder how you ever could have thought that He didn't care. Or how you could have thought of Him at times as an impersonal Savior. Now it is just you and Him, one on one, and there's not another soul in sight. He is as real and personable as anyone you have ever known and He loves you more than they possibly could.

The hand on your shoulder still bears the mark of that fateful day—the day your sins drove that nail through its tender flesh. Yet you feel no lingering guilt, no nagging "if only"s. Jesus is not One to remind you and condemn you for what your sin did, but rather He promised to forgive you and to completely cleanse you from all unrighteousness (see 1 John 1:9). He even went a step further and promised that He would remember your sins "no more" (Hebrews 10:17). They are gone—cast "into the depths of the sea" (Micah 7:19). Having put on His righteousness, you are accounted as if you had never sinned. Is this justice? Not at all. God's mercy withheld the justice you deserved and instead gave you pardon. But was justice done away with or simply forgotten? Not in the slightest. The sentence still had to be paid in its fullness; God's unchanging justice called for this. But the full price fell upon the One who now walks beside you in this meadow—the One who is bringing you to your land which you possess because of His sacrifice.

He waves that nail-scarred hand forward and reveals that your land is just over this next hill. The fact that He created it with you in mind is so typical of your Savior—always thinking about the welfare of His children. Ownership of the land is so trivial in comparison with the prize of getting to spend an eternity with Him. You cannot take your eyes off Him as you make your way toward the top of the hill. His face just radiates with love and He makes every other friend seem like a stranger by comparison.

At the top of the ridge your eyes fall upon the land that has been purchased and designed for you. As perfect and beautiful as all of the rest of this new earth has been, this view tops everything! Your mind, created by this Man beside you, is magnetically drawn to the landscape in front of you which He also created. A perfect match!

The hilly prairie that rolls out before you is covered with wildflowers of every kind, and thousands of butterflies flit from petal to petal. Jesus explains that your land stretches out farther than your eyes can see, and His plan is to show you around the entire terrain. The idea of a continued private walk thrills your heart much more than the prospect of all of this land that you have inherited.

As you stroll across the prairie, you reach down now and then and pick a few of your new wildflowers, which will never die. Theirs is the most wonderful scent you have ever experienced and it seems to energize you more with each breath. Some of these hills possess a surreal familiarity. Perhaps you had dreamed about such a place once as a child, and of course Christ knew that.

You reach the crest of yet another ridge which reveals a large valley complete with a gorgeous, winding river. The light of God sparkles off the river as a small bear scampers out and shakes the water off. Beyond this scene is a lofty mountain range decorated with several waterfalls. This must have been visible in the distance all along, but your attention has been captivated by all the other sights until now. Jesus explains that yes, even the mountains are given to you, and the forest that lines their base, as well.

Sensations of gratitude and love again wash over you as you look once more at the Savior. His own eyes have been on you, for He delights in watching your reaction to His gifts. You are His precious jewel, His child, one created in His own image. This bond that you have will only grow stronger with every walk you share on this beautiful new land.

You fall at His feet in adoration, but He lifts you up and embraces you. You're home now. Forever to live in peace and safety. Again you wonder how you could have ever doubted this loving One who holds you. He leads you down the hill to taste the water from your river. He still has much to show you, and He's eager to see your reaction. Together you walk toward the river and He starts to sing one of your favorite new earth hymns. The song is all about love—a love that will grow through all eternity.

"And they shall build houses, and inhabit them; they shall plant vineyards and eat the fruit of them." —Isaiah 65:21

The Bible makes it very clear that not only will we have a home in the New Jerusalem built by Christ (John 14:2,3; Hebrews 11:16; Revelation 21:2), but we will also have the opportunity to build our own homes out in the country where we can plant vineyards and fruit trees and gardens and anything else we desire.

Owning a home is a dream that millions of people will never realize in this old world. Hard working though they may be, the money just never seems to be quite sufficient for the actual purchase of a house. And even among those who are fortunate enough to buy a home, only a small percentage enjoy the experience of actually designing it themselves and building it to meet those specifications.

Often we read about people in the news who have inherited some grand estate upon the death of a loved one and we tend to think less about their loss, and more about their great gain. Sadly this is frequently the case with our visions of heaven as well. We love to imagine all of the things that we will receive without considering the ultimate cost to the Savior. This is not to say that Christ wants us to be gloomy and despondent all of the time. Quite the opposite. When we contemplate just how undeserving we are and couple that with how gracious He is, our joy and gratitude will noticeably shine forth to all our acquaintances. To whom much is forgiven, the same loves Jesus much (Luke 7:47). But when we consider the sin that cost Jesus His life, and just how dangerous and deadly it really is, we won't be quite so willing to play with it and regard it as a small matter. If Jesus is truly our Friend (and only His friends will be there: John 17:3; 15:14,15), then we will never ignore the great Sacrifice only to dwell upon the inheritance.

It would be well for us to spend some quiet time every day in contemplation of what Jesus did in our behalf, especially the final scenes of His life. Then the best part of thinking about our heavenly home becomes the anticipation of Jesus coming by often to visit us in that very place. Friendship is a wonderful thing indeed, and love is even greater. For all eternity we will testify to the fact that "Greater love hath no man than this, that a man lay down his life for his friends" (John 15:13). And "there is a friend that sticketh closer than a brother" (Proverbs 18:24). That Friend will always be Jesus.

❖ ❖ ❖

You have surveyed your land several times and are choosing the best place to build. The Holy Spirit seems to be impressing you of a certain spot and as your eyes stop there you can just imagine the layout in your mind's eye. Yes, yes indeed this is the place. This gentle hill is slightly higher than the others, and its level top is wide and accommodating. This spot will offer a 360 degree view of the land.

Your plans have all been drawn out, but not on primitive paper. They are recorded in your mind, for your memory is flawless and does not dim over time. You know the exact dimensions of the floor plans and you decide that without a doubt this is the spot to begin. But these projects are always joint ventures. You have spent much of your time helping some of your friends construct their own houses. The joy comes from an entire group getting together, singing praises to God, and watching the thing go up as a team. Last week, in fact, you put the finishing touches on one friend's place and the whole gang agreed to come to your land today and start all over. Working together, to help a friend's house plans come to fruition has not only provided a wonderful chance for fellowship, but has also given you fresh ideas for your own home.

After much anticipation, finally that time has come, and several of your closest friends arrive. You explain your design to them and they are all anxious to see this marvelous house completed. You explain that they are of course welcome to help themselves to all of your fruit trees and anything else they find on your land. More and more friends arrive, and the project finally begins. As the days go by, your house begins to transform from design to reality, and at each stage you are more eager to see the final product. During this period you still have friends' homes in the works, and you take turns on each place. Each of your friends have some of the same people helping, but also others that they know. Thus with each undertaking you make new friends, who then join your project. Each group is constantly growing as the friends multiply.

Now the day has come for your own place to be finished. The gang that started off as several dozen has now grown to several hundred. Each one of these people has become a close friend, and pretty soon you will help some of them start their homes.

Jesus Himself is present for this event. He stands by the front door and the two of you look out over the vast crowd that has come for the completion and housewarming. You invited Him here, and you want to give Him the first tour.

Together you enter your new house and you immediately show Him the special chair that you have designed just for Him. Only He is to sit in that spot and you hope to have it occupied as often as possible.

Again you are oblivious to the things around you as you walk in His presence. The house means nothing to you if not for a place to invite your King.

A train of guests follows you on your tour and they notice that each room contains something in honor of your Lord. The entire house is one giant tribute to the grace that He has provided and an expression of gratitude for His love. Through all eternity you want future visitors to witness and share in your praise to His name.

Having explored all three floors, you and Christ exit the home and talk to the celebrating folks all around. Not only are people there, but your guardian angel and a host of his angel friends have come to join the festival.

Before departing, several friends remind you that when you decide to add on, just let them know and they'll be happy to help. Giving is the spirit that pervades the population of this new earth. That which constantly fills the minds of all is love for God and for each other. Service to others and laying aside self are common attributes here.

As the crowd gradually disperses, not one shred of trash appears anywhere. Nothing looks junky or misused in any way. In fact, each person brought something for either the house or the land, and the estate is actually more attractive now than it was before anyone showed up.

The last friend says goodbye and you and the Savior walk back into your new home. You want Him to stay as long as possible, for you love talking with your best Friend. You treasure just being in His presence. Besides, there's a brand new chair in your living room that's just waiting to be occupied.

"And it shall come to pass, that before they call, I will answer; and while they are yet speaking, I will hear." —Isaiah 65:24

The Lord longs to give us more good gifts than we could ever imagine (Matt. 7:11). The only reason God created all of the beings of the universe was so that He could experience a love relationship with them and shower them with blessings. There is nothing He delights in more than seeing His children happy. But so often the things that we think will make us happy would really not be in our best interest. When we get to heaven our minds will be sanctified, and our requests won't be tainted with selfishness. We will always ask according to God's will and we have the promise that anything asked in harmony with His will is granted (see 1 John 5:14,15). In that day God will be able to say Yes to all of our requests, knowing that none of them could possibly lead to anything that would cause us to stumble.

Isaiah 65:24 tells us that in heaven God will actually answer our prayers before we even ask them. The Lord knows our thoughts and can see the future. He knows what we are about to desire before we even desire it. Therefore if you were in a certain part of His endless universe and you suddenly wanted to be in the presence of God's throne, you could instantly be there at the speed of a thought. God will answer that request before you even get the words out. Impossible you say? With God all things are possible (Mark 10:27). Science fiction you say? The Lord has already performed this miracle in the case of the disciple Philip. Read about how God instantly transported Philip from a pool of water between Jerusalem and Gaza to a city miles away called Azotus (see Acts 8:26-40). Our heavenly Father is truly able to do more than we could ever ask or think (see Ephesians 3:20)!

❖ ❖ ❖

You are exploring the mammoth base of a beautiful, winding canyon. God's handiwork is ever before you and you are constantly learning more about His power through observing His designs. Various rock formations line the edges of the canyon, and you are sitting atop one whose massive, colorful arches caught your eye. You recently started a rock collection, and now you are finding all sorts of specimens to add to your display at home. Gold and silver are commonplace, but now you are finding stones that you've never seen before. In the old earth there were 103 known elements that made up all matter. But here the number of elements are endless, and your heavenly Father is continuously making more, simply by speaking the Word: the transparent gold of the streets being one example.

In your hand is one particularly beautiful and radiant stone. It seems to be filled with tiny mirrors which make the stone appear to take on different shapes and sizes, depending upon the angle at which it is viewed. This has got to be one of the most amazing rocks you have found to date! You are anxious to get it back to your home and place it beside the others. But first you want to talk to your Father about how He created such a thing, and find out more about the science involved here. You think that you would like to be in His presence at the top of the New Jerusalem, and you have faith that you will be.

Instantly you are before the dazzling throne of light and you reverently bow in love as you approach the Creator. You then hold up the rock and your Father smiles. He of course knows that you enjoy and collect these things, and He explains that He had placed that one there just for you. Lovingly and patiently He explains the science behind this rock and as your mind begins to grasp the concept your admiration for Him increases. How wonderful is the God you serve! He never tires of explaining new discoveries, and your love for Him will continue to grow throughout the ceaseless ages. How blessed you are, to be able to call Him "Father."

You remain by His throne for a period of time that escapes your concept. Time in His presence is irrelevant. There is nothing you enjoy more than just being with Him.

He tells you He has a surprise for you at your home, and you eagerly think of going there. Instantly you are at your country home in your rock collection room. Each of the thousands of rocks has its own story to tell. Each was the result of one of your exciting expeditions. Each only helps to reveal more clearly the infinite mind and creativity of your Father. You see a perfect spot for your new stone, and you place it there as its image settles into an oval shape. The light from the window engulfs the stone and bursts forth onto the walls, outshining the reflections of all the other stones.

Now your eyes discover the surprise your Father had waiting for you. At the base of the collection sits a beautiful red stone. As you look more closely, however, you realize that this is in fact half of a cut stone. The stone is ultra light, and its components must contain, among other things, something like helium, for it remains in the air wherever you leave it. Flipping the stone over, you see that it is shaped like a map that reveals where the other half is. Your heart races as you wonder what the Lord has conceived to take place when the two halves are connected.

This map displays an area you have yet to explore. What will this place be like? What kind of creative masterpieces will be in this land? You smile, for you know that wherever it is, the answer is just a thought away.

"They shall plant vineyards and eat the fruit of them...mine elect shall long enjoy the work of their hands."

—Isaiah 65:21,22

As we have seen, the Lord knows exactly what type of land would best suit you. But He won't just place you upon it for you to remain idle and become bored. Long will you enjoy the work of your hands. As you work the land it will be nothing like the way people toil and sweat today. It will be a refreshing and creative venture, increasingly fulfilling. It was after Adam and Eve disobeyed that the ground was cursed. The Lord said, "Cursed is the ground for thy sake; in sorrow shalt thou eat of it all the days of thy life; thorns and thistles shall it bring forth to thee.... In the sweat of thy face shalt thou eat bread" (Genesis 3:17-19).

These thorns, thistles, and weeds of every kind have been a burden to everyone who has worked the land since that fateful day. The battle with the weed still continues. Weeds thrive in the most unfavorable conditions and seem to assault any attempt at a landscaped lawn or flower garden. Throughout the Bible, we see that thorns are a constant reminder and symbol of sin itself (see Matthew 13:7,22; 27:29; Hebrews 6:8; Proverbs 22:5). Working the land today, although rewarding, definitely has its share of frustrations.

As it was before the fall, so shall it be after the new Creation. To work the land will then bring us utter joy and satisfaction. And the land itself will no longer produce those pesky weeds, thorns, and thistles. No, in the new earth the land will cooperate with our efforts to the fullest.

Besides the vineyards spoken of in Scripture, there will no doubt be opportunities to work with whatever plant life your heart desires. Cultivate a garden filled with all your favorite foods. Plant as many trees as you want, whatever variety you like. There will be no fear of any species not thriving in your part of the world, for there will be no death in the new earth, and that includes the trees. And sprinkler systems will forever be a thing of the past. No plant there will suffer from lack of water, for the living water from the throne of God will continually refresh the entire planet. Everything in sight will be vibrant and healthy.

Finally, the land itself can be altered by you. Do you wish to divert a new creek off of that broad river? Go ahead. Do you want to dig a tunnel through part of your mountains? Feel free. Or how about an island in the middle of that lake? You can do whatever you please. The land has been given to you, and unlike the land of the old earth, it can never be taken away.

❖ ❖ ❖

You are admiring the beautiful new color of the sky as you finish planting the honeysuckle bush along the grove of trees by a tiny pond. It reminds you of those rare sunsets on the old earth when the sky just radiated with streaks of pink and orange. Your God is certainly a God of infinite creativity, and He is constantly revealing new and beautiful gifts to His children. You think about that friend who came by to visit a while back, and you remember how you had agreed that this particular hue was one of your favorites. You wonder if she is beholding the sky now and receiving this same blessing.

The land itself rivals the beauty of the sky and you pause to take in the scene. Trees, shrubs, and wildflowers of endless variety adorn the land with vivid color. While the freshness of spring is ever before you, the brilliance of autumn splashes over every red and golden leaf.

Leaning down to the honeysuckle you take a deep breath and savor the aroma. The fragrance is mild and sweet, yet invigorating. It occurs to you that although you never grow tired in the new earth, there are certain things, like this honeysuckle fragrance, that seem to energize you even more. You wonder if your energy level is actually increasing all the time and will continue to increase throughout eternity. You will definitely ask your Father about this one.

The tiny pond beside the honeysuckle is the home to several turtles which you have named, as well as multitudes of bright, colorful fish, and a family of black and brown ducks. This is one of your favorite spots to bring visitors. It is quiet and calm, and the ducks just love the attention. No matter what you and your guests talk about here, the subject always turns to Jesus. Your admiration for Him has been growing with each new discovery, and His love seems to be revealed more clearly with the passing of time. The Cross of Calvary is your science and your song; His sacrifice, a mystery constantly unfolding to your mind.

A mile away from the pond lies the garden, loaded with your favorite delicacies. Your eyes scan the progress as you approach this natural grocery store. On either side of the garden are the fruit trees. Large, plump cherries, apples, peaches, dates, figs, and the rest of your favorite fruits cover the trees and await your picking. Their scent drifts through the garden on a gentle breeze. Along the far edge of the orchard are the bushes and vines. Giant blackberries, blueberries, raspberries, and other such treats almost obscure the bushes with their ample clusters. Their luscious taste reminds you of that homemade pie you used to eat, only much more flavorful. And these treats require no added sugar, and will never clog your arteries. Then of course there are the grapevines. From these you make as much refreshing grape juice as you or your friends could ever want. Even Christ has shared this "fruit of the vine" with you on numerous occasions.

You even have a few vanilla plants for some of your favorite recipes. Several maple trees also produce their syrup for a luscious maple bread that is a favorite in these parts. And the honeybees have provided their golden treat in several hives among the trees. You often enjoy watching these diligent creatures fly from flower to flower as they carry on their work. And now you have no fear of that infamous sting.

At your feet in the garden you notice an immense, green-striped watermelon. You feel it and thump it to make sure it is ripe. Satisfied that it's ready for consumption, you crack it open on a nearby stone and then break off a tiny piece for a test. This refreshing, cool flavor cannot be compared to any melon you tasted in the old earth. In fact, it's even better than your last melon here! Is the food also getting better with time, or is your appreciation level simply expanding? Perhaps your taste buds are constantly improving. Whatever the reason, every meal you have seems better than the last.

You lift half of the melon and start heading toward home, leaving the other half for your cousin who had said he wanted to see your garden and is coming by a little later. There is no fear of the luscious fruit drying out in the open air, or being destroyed by bugs. When you come back to this spot the melon will still be as fresh as when you first cracked it open.

Nearing your home, you cross the bridge that you built over your circle-creek. A while back you had decided that you would like to have a creek flowing in a continuous giant circle all the way around your house. You designed and created a large channel that ultimately formed this circle about a quarter-mile out from the perimeter of your home. Then you diverted some water from one of your rivers into the new creek. Knowing that with God all things are possible, you studied the science of perpetual motion, and trusted in God to make it happen. Once the water flowed into the channel, by the power of God it didn't just form a donut-shaped lake, but rather flowed on continuously in this formation. Many of your guests have enjoyed swimming or just floating in the circle-creek and you love to watch their expressions when they first see it.

God's power can also make the rivers flow uphill, and you have already designed an area on one of your highest mountains that allows for just that. You see it on the horizon as you walk up the marble stairs to your front door: three giant rivers that actually flow up to the top of the lofty mount, and then separate in different courses. One river turns left and snakes along the top of the mountain range. Giant trees of various sorts line either side of this river, giving it extra beauty. You chose and planted exactly the trees you thought should go there. The second river cascades down the other side of the mountain at a perfect 45 degree angle creating acres of white water and a cool mist. The third river actually arcs up into the air about 100 feet beyond the peak and then crashes down into a giant lake. All three rivers can transport people to the top, and guests choose which ride they would like to try.

Each design and project you undertake is done so with only two things in mind: glorifying the love and power of God, and bringing joy to your fellow human beings.

Before entering your house, you stop and relax in a comfy chair which sits between two of the front pillars. From here you can see almost all of your land, and the pink streaks in the sky are giving way to a shimmering gold. Another cool bite of watermelon fills your mouth as you lean back and contemplate the Creator of all things. From the wonderful food in your mouth to the marble on which your feet rest; from the mountain range that graces the horizon, to the very sky that shimmers in dazzling color; all have come from the hand of your best Friend and Redeemer. You truly serve a mighty God.

"Dost thou know...the wondrous works of him which is perfect in knowledge?" —Job 37:16

"[He] doeth great things past finding out; yea, and wonders without number." —Job 9:10

When I was in school, I must admit there were few things I found less appealing than biology. The idea of cutting open a dead frog and having to learn the names of all those foul-smelling parts was not my idea of a good time. One thing I did discover, however, was that there was, without exception, a design involved in every aspect of animal, mineral, and plant life. It seemed that no matter how small the object—even under a microscope—an organized, elaborate plan was evident.

When we consider the incredible variety of life forms that cover planet earth, we begin to realize just how many intricate, unique systems must be involved in the inner workings of these entities.

In the beginning Adam and Eve were constantly witnessing their Lord's perfection and creativity apparent in all of His handiwork. Every living thing attested to the infinite wisdom of its Creator. The opportunity to study nature up close and uncover the secrets concealed therein was one of the greatest blessings bestowed upon the first couple. Their studies were not hindered by all of the limitations we have today. With perfect minds and superior faculties they were able to learn from nature in ways we can't even begin to imagine: ways we will be experiencing, however, in the world to come. Thus a staunch evolutionist would find no joy in heaven for he would constantly be trying to explain away all of the Master's designs as "accidents." He would forfeit the blessing of seeing the Creator's hand in all of His works.

Consider this fact for a moment: if you were to choose just one item—animal, mineral, or plant—and decided to study it, examining the smaller and smaller components within that object, you could keep yourself busy for all eternity and still never learn all of its secrets. How can this be? Because regardless of how small any portion of matter gets, it can always be cut in half. No matter how many times you split the element, you would never reach an ultimate "foundation" to it all—no starting point. Try to wrap your mind around *that* one.

❖ ❖ ❖

You are taking a walk through the flower garden behind your country home and you come across a beautiful yellow rosebush, the seeds of which you had long ago planted. Charmed by its bright blossoms, you pluck one of the flowers. The fact that all of this beauty was stored within those tiny seeds intrigues you. You decide to examine the contents of one of the remaining seeds. You have no need of a microscope, for ever since you received your new body, all of your senses are infinitely keener than the most powerful human inventions of old earth. You simply adjust your eyes and begin to observe the wonders of this complex thing called a seed. Your eyes now increase their magnification as you begin to study the very cells that make up the inner components of the seed. You marvel at the detail and intricacy of such a tiny, tiny thing.

You have just begun another journey into inner space. Just as the Creator's universe has no end, no matter how far out you journey, this inner universe has no end (or rather, beginning) no matter how far *in* you go. Since there are no time schedules to adhere to, you decide to continue your journey down into the universe of this rose seed.

You can stop at any stage inward and look around in detail, or zoom in at high speed and watch the stages pass before you in rapid succession. You have done this before with other plants and animals and some of this looks familiar to you. It is an education all in itself to learn and compare the inner workings of a variety of life forms, each revealing the perfect plan laid out by God in all He touches.

Now you allow your eyes to zoom in faster and further than you ever have before and you find yourself in a strange, new world. These bits of matter, now 100 trillion times smaller than an atom, are completely new to you and the design is a beautiful thing to behold. You pause for a moment to take in the scene. No need to take any notes, for your memory is flawless and in 100 billion millennia from now you will be able to recall every one of these scenes in perfect detail. As you observe the complex system, you again realize the truth in the statement that God's ways are "past finding out" (Job 9:10), for you understand that there is no end to this matter-splitting study. The Creator is so infinite in time, dimension and wisdom that He was there before you, designing even these infinitesimal life-support stages, although they themselves have no starting point! He created the systems that support these, and the systems that support those, and so on for infinity. Now *that* is an awesome God!

With the distant ringing of your door chimes, you realize that you have a visitor. No problem: you simply set your focus so that it will automatically return to this stage of micro-vision when you resume your study. You turn from the flower garden to go greet your guest. As you contemplate the wisdom and power of your Creator, you know that you will have lots of new things to share with your visitor. Perhaps this person will join you on your next incredible journey through the living kaleidoscope of God's creation: a journey into the boundless universe of inner space.

"And I say unto you, That many shall come from the east and west, and shall sit down with Abraham, and Isaac, and Jacob, in the kingdom of heaven." —Matthew 8:11

Have you ever wanted to ask one of the characters in the Bible a certain question? Perhaps ask them why they did or didn't do a certain thing? What was it like for Noah and his family to be completely alone on the earth after the flood? When Adam and Eve were cast out of Eden, how often did they go back to the entrance of the Garden and peer past the flaming sword at their former home? What was it like for Mary to actually give birth to and raise Jesus?

Well, when you get to heaven you can ask them. The friendships you will have with the Bible heroes might even be closer than any relationship they may have had on earth. How can this be? Because you will have all eternity for your friendship with Joseph to grow. Your love for your dear friend Esther will continually increase. And as the ages roll on, you will become more and more familiar with the personality of David.

Yes, the Lord promises us that we will have plenty of opportunities to speak to and build relationships with Bible characters. Your voice will unite with theirs as you sing the glorious praises of the One who made it possible.

❖ ❖ ❖

Daniel and you are walking along a massive, golden bridge which spans one of the new earth's large rivers. The two of you are on your way to the Great Throne Room of the Father and the Lamb in the New Jerusalem. You have many friends in this place, but somehow you and Daniel seem to have an extra special friendship. Many times you have discussed his visions recorded in the book of the Bible which bears his name. How thankful you are that he was true to his post, and faithfully recorded what he was shown. The role that he was assigned during his allotted time on the earth was carried out faithfully by the grace of God. One of the things that has become extremely clear to you since you arrived here is the fact that everyone who was ever born on planet earth had a specific plan for their life. The tragic part is that so few ever sought to know from God what that plan was. But those who did, always found. The Savior had made this perfectly clear in Matthew 7:7: a promise you still cherish even today.

Although your sinful record was erased by God, and you can no longer bring those sins to memory, you do know that much of your life had been wasted before you allowed Jesus to really take control. You had made many professions of faith but they were all shallow until you fully grasped the need for complete and utter surrender to Him. The Lord in His wonderful mercy had then fulfilled His promise to show you His will for your life and eventually your path was made known. He had strengthened you to redeem the time and carry out His specific plan for you.

Now Daniel and you are once again discussing this very topic. How amazing is God, you declare, to have worked through such unworthy vessels. You are relieved that it's not constantly lorded over you that Daniel's life was spotted with far less sin than your own. No condescension takes place in this land, for all are aware of their own unworthiness. Christ accepted you at your new birth as though you had no spotted past and as if you had literally been born at that moment. Thus there is no asterisk placed by your name in the books of heaven reading *Barely Made It, or *Forgiven, But Reluctantly So. No, the Lord had taken you where you were, and started afresh. He delighted in His mercy toward you, and kept His eyes on you and your future with Him. You and Daniel cannot stop talking about your love for Jesus and His love for the two of you. You still can't fully grasp how Christ was able to literally take your sins upon Himself and clean up the record as if you lived His perfect life, but you intend to study the Plan of Salvation some more today when you reach the New Jerusalem.

Floating peacefully downstream beneath you in a heavenly vessel is a friend you met in the Holy City when you first entered its gates. She is a woman who lived during the days of the prophet Samuel, and your personalities just seemed to hit it off. She smiles and waves as she recognizes you. You never dreamed that you would have so many friends here from other time periods on earth. You have discovered that people are people, and the special bond you have with the Savior only binds each friendship even tighter.

Now Daniel and you proceed down the golden steps of the bridge onto the lush, green grass which stretches out for miles at the base of the New Jerusalem. Several angel friends greet you in passing. The soft grass feels warm under your feet as you head toward the hill on which the city sits. As many times as you have come into this city, you never tire of beholding its splendor. The place is so immense that in spite all of your years here, you have yet to see the entire thing. Rooms and roads, alleys and balconies, buildings, bridges, and staircases fill the glorious place and they just never seem to end.

As you approach the Simeon gate on the southern wall, you see the apostle John speaking to an angel. His writings also brought you closer to the Lord, and you have thanked him as well for being faithful to the part he was to play. One of the things you remember about John is that he was extremely interested in speaking to you. He had seen visions—which he faithfully recorded in the book of Revelation—about the people who would be alive at the very end of the world, and here he had been able to speak to you in person. He had asked you all sorts of questions about what it was like to be among the group that went through the great Time of Trouble and were alive at the Second Coming. This is the group to which the people of God had wanted to belong since the ascension of Christ. What a privilege, he had exclaimed, to be among those who gave the final warning to the earth before the return of the Lord! You had always been envious of the Bible characters for the times in which they lived, but you have consistently been told by them that you lived in the most amazing time of all—the last days of the earth.

The beloved apostle grins as he recognizes you. He and Daniel briefly talk once again about the similarities in their visions. The

Lord had used these two men to give the clearest picture to the last generation on earth of what the end would be like. They have a special bond as well.

Passing through the majestic pearl gate, you enter into the busy, golden street. Happy people are milling about the place, some exploring its infinite secrets, some conversing with one another, and some on their way to or from the Great Throne Room. Faces shine from being in the very presence of the Life-giver; from head to toe they gleam with pure energy. An impromptu choir has started to sing over beside one of the great fountains that line the street. They are singing one of your favorite songs and you and Daniel join in as you pass by.

Just stepping down from one of the many giant staircases are Peter and Noah. Peter is asking Noah some questions about the days in which he lived. You are surprised at how many Bible characters were anxious to talk to other Bible characters when they got there. But after all, people are people.

Finally the two of you reach the Great Throne Room and as you enter, you see Adam, the father of the race, on his way out. This is your great-great-multiple-times-grandpa standing here, and you will always have a special place in your heart for him. Everywhere he goes he sees his descendants and he has been determined to develop intimate relationships with all. Suddenly an idea comes to you: you will start with your parents and try to trace your line all the way back to Adam to see if you can locate all of them here in an unbroken chain. With each preceding generation above you, the possibilities double, so this will make for quite a complex and fun project. You have already met many of your ancestors, which makes this new idea seem even better.

You embrace the tall, handsome figure and Daniel does the same. His fall and all of the woe that he brought into the world by his single act of disobedience is forgotten, cleaned from the record. For 930 years on old earth he witnessed the horrible consequences of disobedience to God. It seemed a great load to bear, but now he sees only joy and happiness: all of it, thanks to the Savior.

Daniel and you approach the throne and bow reverently in the presence of infinite Holiness. You then rise, eager to begin your latest inquiries about the Plan of Salvation. The theme is inexhaustible and grows more and more fascinating as you study it. Love, you have experienced, is not a static thing, but grows and in fact multiplies as it is exercised.

You and the prophet take turns asking questions, which the Father and Son patiently and eloquently answer. What a privilege it is to speak to the Deity face to face! And what a blessing it is to be asking your questions with a man you once only read about in the Old Testament: a man whom you now call "friend."

"They that go down to the sea in ships, that do business in great waters; These see the works of the Lord, and his wonders in the deep." —Psalm 107:23, 24

The prophet John saw the new earth in vision and declared that "there was no more sea" (Revelation 21:1). This was most likely the case before the flood, as well. When God destroyed the world with a flood, it involved more than a simple 40 day rainstorm. The Bible testifies that "the same day were all the fountains of the great deep broken up, and the windows of heaven were opened." This reveals that not only did the water plunge down from the sky, but the bodies of water on earth cracked open in the "great deep" and began to overflow at a tremendous rate. In addition, the water that came from the sky itself had its source in more than mere rain clouds.

In the creation account, we get a glimpse of the Creator at work: "And God said, Let there be a firmament in the midst of the waters, and let it divide the waters from the waters. And God made the firmament, and divided the waters which were under the firmament from the waters which were above the firmament: and it was so" (Genesis 1:6,7).

Many scholars believe this refers to more than just the water content in clouds. It is very likely that there was a far greater amount of water—in fact a layer of water—at the edge of our atmosphere. Before the flood there had been no rain, because "the Lord God had not caused it to rain upon the ground...but there went up a mist from the earth, and watered the whole face of the ground" (Genesis 2:5,6). This is another reason so few of the antediluvians believed Noah's predictions of water falling from the sky; it had never happened before. A mist, or dew had simply formed on the ground every morning and kept everything watered.

Before the flood, consequently, there was not nearly so much uninhabitable land under water as there is today. Between two-thirds and three-fourths of the planet's surface is now covered by the sea. In the new earth it will not be so. But does this mean there won't be any large lakes or sea creatures as we know them today? No more dolphins or sting rays or sea lions? It seems unlikely that God would do away with such marvelous animals simply because there won't be vast oceans covering the land.

I have no doubts that there will be dolphins in the new earth. But according to the Word of God their habitat will not rule the planet as it does today. The world will then be as it was in the beginning: a place created primarily for human habitation. We have no need to wonder if God will prevent us from enjoying the thrill of swimming with the wonderful creatures that now roam our oceans. The giant "seas" may be no more, but His fascinating marine creatures will live on forever.

❖ ❖ ❖

You have just come across one of the mammoth blue lakes that God formed on the new earth. Down below the cliff on which you stand, you see a large pod of sea lions basking on the rocks. A trail a hundred yards away leads down to the water's edge and you notice that the trail is dotted with crabs. You must take a closer look at these creatures on your way to the sea lions. As you start down the path, you pick up one of the crabs, knowing that it won't try to pinch you. Hurting is foreign to this world now, just as it is to the entire universe. A small group of people are also examining the crabs along a distant trail. Not only are you safe from the crabs, but the crabs are safe from careless humans. You and the others only want to look at them and learn more about God's creativity.

You carry your crab down the winding trail which is lined with numerous palm trees. The sand along the path feels warm between your toes as it glistens a gold-speckled white. On the opposite shore you see thousands of dolphins jumping out over the sparkling, blue water, with a few playful seals and a large group of people swimming among them.

As you approach the sea lions, five or six of them hobble over to see you. They bark loudly as if competing for your attention. You set the crab down and one of the sea lions curiously follows after it. Other sea lions are having a ball diving into the water, and it looks so refreshing that you walk out to the edge of the rocks and jump right in.

As you splash through the surface, the underwater scenery just explodes with color. The water here is about 50 feet deep and it is just as light and clear at the bottom as it is by the surface. Fish of countless varieties swim past while the sea lions chase each other. The coral formations below are breathtaking, and you quickly swim on down to take a closer look.

Three or four eels stick their heads out of their holes and you confidently reach out and pet them. One exits its hole and swims past an octopus along the bright coral reef. Several gorgeous blue sharks now catch your eye as they glide peacefully over the top of the reef. You turn east and scan the distance. In the old earth a distant view underwater would be a contradiction in terms, but here you marvel at how far you can see with perfect clarity. This is the narrowest part of the lake and your view extends all the way to the eastern shore: several miles off, you estimate. There you again see the folks swimming with the dolphins.

To the north lies the Colossal Reef—the most famous part of these waters. It is the largest coral reef in this hemisphere, towering over everything in sight, like a colorful band of underwater skyscrapers. It must be well over a thousand feet tall and stretches out for miles. This magnificent living structure is just teeming with marine life. The octopus, sea urchin, squid, jellyfish, giant clam, sea turtle, barracuda, starfish and innumerable other creatures have made this their home. Thick schools of vibrant fish flow in all directions, some forming giant, living spirals. Hundreds of people swim all about the reef on every level. Even at these depths, the distant Light from the Holy City permeates every square inch clear down to the sandy bottom.

As you swim closer, you begin to recognize some of the people. A few of them are marine enthusiasts, and they can almost always be found exploring the underwater depths. A handful of them you met during various house-raising projects; some have even been to your home. All have come to witness the majestic works of the Creator.

Three sea lions from the shore have kept up with you, and one of them examines a giant school of luminescent jellyfish up near the surface. His idea is a good one, and soon you find yourself encompassed by a pulsating cloud of these strange but beautiful, glowing creatures.

Eventually the cloud drifts across the top of the reef to the other side, where you notice a giant humpback whale heading toward the surface. You must examine this masterpiece up close, so you head toward the mammoth creature, sea lions still in tow.

With several mighty swoops of that giant tail, the whale launches himself out of the water, breaches 50 feet in the air right in front of you, and crashes back down into the water. Never before have you witnessed such a sight live, up close, and with absolutely no fear of danger.

Swimming along beside him, you grab one of his massive fins and follow him up out of the water as he breaches again. The fresh air blasting the cool water on your skin is exhilarating and together you plunge back in for more. This time you grab the whale's tail and hang on for the ride of your life! Two of the sea lions are still with you, and they now seem to be racing with the whale.

Ultimately the whale takes you near a cove where you let go and watch him as he heads back out into the crystal clear depths. You decide to swim into the cove where the water is shallow again. A handful of sting rays glide past and the bright reflection of the water's surface dances off their backs. These creatures look as though they are flying through the water and you feel right at home as you soar freely among them. You reach out and feel one of their "wings." Its skin is velvety smooth. How endless is the variety of creatures in your Father's repertoire!

On the shore of the cove you spot several of your friends enjoying a drink together. The water here is now shallow enough for walking, and they call you over as you come up onto the beach. One persistent sea lion has followed you for your entire journey and he waddles onto the shore with you. Your friends not only hand you a refreshing fruit smoothie, but they toss your whiskered buddy a handful of fruit which immediately disappears. You sit back and enjoy the gorgeous view with your friends as the lofty palm trees wave quietly overhead in the tropical breeze. You begin to discuss some of your discoveries, and several questions arise that you want to bring to your Father. After this drink, the entire group will go before His throne and thank Him again for the beautiful world He made for you. Then you will present your questions about some of His amazing creatures.

A crab scampers over your toes as you take another sip of your drink. Throughout all eternity you can experience the works of the Master Designer and His "wonders in the deep." Praise be His holy name!

"Make a joyful noise unto the Lord, all ye lands. Serve the Lord with gladness: come before his presence with singing."
—Psalm 100:1, 2

We live in a world that often creates clichés about things that are not well understood. One example of this is the view many people hold about heaven. The most popular cliché in this regard is the image of the halo-capped, winged saint sitting on a cloud and strumming a three-stringed harp. No wonder so many people would rather live for this world than for the world to come! If the cliché were even close to reality, eternity would be boring. Imagine spending all your days looking over the edge of a cloud and having only the sound of an occasional harp string to lift your spirits. The Enemy of truth knows that this scenario has no appeal to the human mind and thus he creates such false ideas of heaven to keep us from caring whether or not we ever live there. When we are tempted to look to the allurements of this world we would do well to remember that "Faith is the substance of things hoped for, the evidence of things not seen" (Hebrews 11:1).

In reality, the harps that we receive will be unlike anything we have ever seen or played. The sound which they produce will be more beautiful than anything we can imagine. Now multiply that times all those in the great multitude of the redeemed and mix it with the glorious sound of the innumerable angels. If you have ever had chills run down your spine at the singing of the national anthem or the playing of a powerful composition, you have only begun to taste a fraction of what the music in heaven will be like. All will be given the ability to play these instruments, and there should be no doubt that countless other instruments will be available as well.

In this world we have created a seemingly endless collection of songs from the chromatic scale, consisting of only 12 tones or notes (with the exception of Oriental music). A transformed, heavenly mind would be able to come up with millions of new songs from those same notes; but what would such a mind be able to do with, say 20 notes? Or 100 notes? And what about a million notes, with a million new instruments on which to play those notes? If God wanted to He could constantly be creating more notes for all eternity, and thus the possibilities would be inexhaustible.

Yes, the music in heaven will be an entirely new experience for the redeemed. As they join in song and praise with the angels, their hearts will be lifted to an even higher plane. They can sing as loud as they want, and nobody ever misses a note or sings out of key. The world's biggest choir will fill the streets of the Holy City with the sound of their voices and with the strumming of those illustrious, glittering harps.

❖ ❖ ❖

You have taken your place among the great choir of the redeemed. Although you have participated many times, you still never cease to be amazed at the vastness of the assembly. It is a special time: a time to meet friends and to unite in one majestic hymn after another. These hymns are sung with more enthusiasm than in any of the church services in the old earth, yet they lack the clamor and irreverence which had marked some assemblies. New hymns are constantly being written, and as each one is introduced, you all agree that surely this is the best one ever. Then when you go back and sing a previous hymn you decide that maybe that one was actually the best. Today you are given the chance to introduce your latest song. It has been a while since you wrote a song, but recently as you walked across your land, your love for Jesus caused you to spring forth in praise which then developed into a song. In the old earth you had absolutely no song writing talents. You dabbled in poetry once in a while in school, but to write down notes in a way that would eventually be catchy to those who heard them was beyond your abilities. You always had a real admiration for songwriters and an insatiable love for music.

First up is a friend that you knew in the old earth since childhood. She walks to the throne of God and the Lamb, and bows in reverence as silence fills the assembly. Although she speaks now to her Savior in words just above a whisper, the acoustics are designed so that all can hear quite clearly. She tenderly explains that this song came to her while walking with Jesus through the City gates one day. His smile radiates as He hears her story. This is His precious daughter, and this song will be very special to His heart.

You smile as you watch your longtime friend—once so shy, timid, and somewhat clumsy, now beautiful and graceful—preparing to perform for the Majesty of the universe. She is so dear to your heart. How grateful you are that through accepting Christ, this relationship could continue in Paradise.

She lifts her golden harp, and the first note breaks the silence. You and the great multitude all listen with pleasure, and will join her on the second stanza. The song is truly beautiful and you prepare to join the melody. The solo explodes into an enormous orchestration of sound that seems to electrify the air. Several million violin-type instruments add depth to the masterpiece, while the flutes and other pipes cover the high end. Trumpets give the song a royal tone as the harps of the redeemed control the melody. Voices from all those assembled drift up from the planet, and the headquarters of the universe overflows with this awesome song.

Ecstasy fills your soul and your praises to God become louder and more powerful. You never want this song to end, and the music seems to course right through your veins.

But finally that last high note is reached, and the mighty orchestra and choir bring the song to a close. Praise to God fills the city as Jesus stands beside your friend and hugs her tight against His broad chest. Everything she has, He has given her. All of her musical abilities are a gift from Him. And yet He is greatly appreciative of her expression of love.

As you step out of your place and begin to make your way down one of the silver aisles you decide to give her a hug on her way up. Praises to God continue to rise from the assembly as your paths meet. Harp still in hand, she throws her arms around you, and you both know that words need not be spoken.

She then makes her way up her aisle as you approach the Creator. You bow reverently and then proceed to tell the story of your own song. The expressions of the Father and Son reveal that your story is precious to them.

You then strike the first note of your latest tribute to the King. Within moments the entire city—all of the redeemed who have ever lived, and all of the angels—will burst forth with the song that you yourself wrote: a song that doesn't even begin to express how you truly feel.

"There is a river, the streams whereof shall make glad the city of God" —Psalm 46:4

One of the most exhilarating things to do that is both fun and a great way to view God's handiwork is white water rafting. When I was growing up in Tennessee, we used to take visitors to a river called the Hiwasee. It was great fun to go down this river in either a raft or more commonly, inner tubes. The Hiwasee was obviously not as rough as other rivers in the area, or inner tubes would not have been allowed. But we enjoyed the calm parts almost as much as the rough. There were several drawbacks, however, that we will not have to face in the new earth.

For one thing, we had to drive quite a distance just to get to this river. Secondly, we had to pay for the experience. Also the water was perpetually cold, even in the middle of July, and those first few minutes were always agonizing. Relief only came when we simply froze and became numb, unable to feel anything (except for a few jutting rocks!). Then there was the inevitable burnt skin from four hours of sun and washed off sunscreen. And finally, the sores that invariably popped up under our arms from trying to steer our tubes the entire time. I'm glad God has a better way!

❖ ❖ ❖

You have jumped into one of the enormous rivers that flow out of the New Jerusalem and span the far ends of the earth. This part of the river is full of people who, like yourself, are enjoying the ride. The water is the perfect temperature, and you have no need to change into a bathing suit. The robe of light that covers you is designed to work efficiently in any circumstance imaginable.

Cheerful laughter is all around you, and you smile as you see a couple of guys try different ways of floating. With each fork in the river, groups are separated. Some are headed to their country homes. Others are destined for parts of the earth where they are undertaking diverse group projects. Still others are headed out to various giant lakes to view the marine life. And some, like yourself, are simply charting new courses along the river that they have never experienced before.

In the past you have been in the mood to join large groups as they make their way down the river. Today you feel like going it alone so you can focus on nothing but nature. There goes the channel that heads toward your country home. You pass it by, for you have only begun to explore.

You guide yourself into a branch you've never been down before, and it winds its way through a lush, hilly landscape. At times the water turns white, and you enjoy the ride as you safely plunge through the foam without a raft or tube. It is impossible for you to be injured in any way.

You now dip below the surface to take in this underwater world. A half-dozen otters playfully swim by in the crystal clear depths, and you laugh as you witness their antics. The riverbed down here is gorgeous! Words cannot describe what a glorious home have the animals in the earth made new.

As you rise to the surface again, you see that this part of the river is edged with brilliant wildflowers of all the colors of the rainbow. They seem to shine as they wave in the breeze. The river is passing through a prairie, and the tall, green grass seems to stretch out forever. There's not a soul in sight.

Another dive into the river and you swim to the bottom, exploring some of the gold that caught your eye. No need for staking a claim; it's yours for the taking. You decide two nuggets are enough, as a memento of this joyful trip.

Now back to the surface and you're in a forest. Bears are all along the river's edge and a couple of them even dive in playfully. You grab onto the back of one and he takes you for a quick ride before crawling out on the opposite side.

As you exit the forest, a hundred-story waterfall awaits you, and you thrill as you plunge over its edge! The impact into the crystal pool below drives you down toward the bottom, where you witness a family of large turtles making their way across the bright, sandy floor.

As the current pulls you on downstream, again you enjoy some white water before the river settles into a quiet calm. You float on your back as you relax and let the stream take you where it will. You see a beautiful valley down below and wonder what surprises are in store for you there. You will soon find out, for your journey has just begun.

"But they that wait upon the Lord shall renew their strength; they shall mount up with wings as eagles; they shall run, and not be weary; and they shall walk, and not faint." —Isaiah 40:31

The desire to fly has been an inherent part of humanity throughout the ages. Ancient drawings and writings reveal that mankind has always contemplated various ways to achieve this seemingly illusive dream. After thousands of years and innumerable failures, human beings finally got their first real taste of flight in a place called Kitty Hawk. On December 17, 1903 the world marveled and cheered at the achievement of Wilbur and Orville Wright. The long awaited dream of human flight was then and henceforth a reality. The following label text was displayed with the original Wright Flyer after it was acquired by the Smithsonian Institution in 1948:

> By Original Scientific Research the Wright Brothers Discovered the Principles of Human Flight. As Inventors, Builders, and Flyers, They Further Developed the Aeroplane, Taught Men to Fly, and Opened the Era of Aviation.

They "taught men to fly" by their research and experimentation, which bore fruit in the first successful self-propelled flying machine. Do you suppose God will do any less in the new earth?

Bible writers themselves showed an interest in flight. King David once declared, "Oh, that I had wings like a dove! for then would I fly away, and be at rest" (Psalm 55:6). And in the Proverbs of wisdom we hear of three things described as "too wonderful for me." The first one listed is: "The way of an eagle in the air" (Proverbs 30:18,19). It has always been hard for any of us to look up at an eagle soaring freely and peacefully above the trees and not wonder what such an experience would be like.

"Delight thyself also in the Lord; and he shall give thee the desires of thine heart" (Psalm 37:4).

Imagine getting to heaven and watching angels fly over the walls of the Holy City. You ask Jesus if you could fly up and join them, and He says that such activities you can never experience. You must take the stairs if you want to get there. Here is the One who said that "with God all things are possible" (Mark 10:27), and now He is limiting you and telling you that this desire of yours is asking too much? Not likely. The Lord will indeed give us the "desires of our hearts" because "the desire of the righteous is only good" (Proverbs 11:23), and "no good thing will He withhold from them that walk uprightly" (Psalm 84:11). But our Lord will go much further than the Wright brothers ever could. He won't limit us to the primitive, bulky framework of an aircraft. Such confining activities would prove utterly boring to us in a universe that holds such limitless possibilities. Granting humans the freedom of solitary flight will not be impossible for Him, and He obviously feels that wings are good enough for angels.

The apostle Paul, under the inspiration of the Holy Spirit, assures us that when Jesus returns in the clouds of glory we will indeed be caught up to meet the resurrected saints in the air as we rise toward Jesus (1 Thessalonians 4:16,17). This will be the first of many flights for the redeemed. If Christ is able to make us airborne then, surely He can do so later.

Once when confronted by the Sadducees over what they considered to be difficulties in the concept of a resurrection and life in heaven, Jesus stated that the redeemed will be "as the angels of God in heaven" (Matthew 22:30). Notice He didn't say that they would "become angels," just that they would be "as," in other words "like" the angels. He was, in this passage, referring to marriage, but nevertheless, it leaves us to wonder what will be the similarities between us and these winged ones we've heard about all our lives.

It would do us well to once again remember Paul's statement that "eye hath not seen, nor ear heard, neither have entered into the heart of man, the things which God hath prepared for them that love him" (1 Corinthians 2:9). No matter what you imagine "wings" to be, they will be entirely different, beyond our present comprehension. No matter what joys and activities you can picture right now, God will not only match, but surpass them a thousand times over (see Ephesians 3:20). Will we be able to fly in heaven? The Wright brothers made it happen in this old world. As for heaven, we know with a certainty that "with God all things are possible."

❖ ❖ ❖

An eagle appears in the top of a giant redwood tree. You have frequently seen this eagle here and have even given her a name. You decide to go to the top of this enormous tree and see the bird up close again. Although climbing is an option, and you in fact enjoy climbing trees, you decide you'd rather fly this time. Your guardian angel stands beside you and he apparently was thinking the same thing, for he stretches out his wings and takes off directly upward. Just for fun, you take off by gliding a foot above the ground at a tremendous speed before ascending. Slowly your altitude rises as you bank toward the east, ultimately turning yourself around and soaring toward the tree.

Your guardian angel is nearly at the nest, and he looks back and motions for you to join him. A few more flaps of your wings and you are just above the top branches, looking for a spot to rest your feet. You see a space between the limbs that can accommodate you, and you lower yourself gently into that spot. The eagle sits calmly in her nest as you land beside her. You stroke her head and she seems to enjoy it. True to character, she rubs her head against your hand, wanting more and more. You laugh as she moves her head to your other hand.

Now you coax her out of the tree by standing up again and walking out onto one of the giant limbs. She knows what this means, for you have done this dozens of times before. Following your lead she comes out of her nest and hops over to the limb beside you and the angel. You look out over the horizon. Nothing but a sea of green treetops for miles and miles; it is a peaceful sight. You are eager to dip in and out of the foliage in a flight that you know will be thrilling. After that you will fly to your house and show your eagle friend some new trees you recently added to your land.

Jumping off the limb, you clear all of the branches and let yourself plunge toward the ground. The free fall is exhilarating! As you near the surface, you suddenly unfold your wings, leveling out your flight, and begin one of your favorite flying exercises. The woods are thick with trees, and you must maneuver yourself from left to right between them at this high speed. Left, right, left, left, right: the trees zip by in flashes. You add a little more excitement to the ride by increasing your altitude among the outstretched branches above. This creates the need to dart up and down as well as side to side, and you feel as though you're blazing through the world's biggest obstacle course. Finally you decide to rise back into the blue expanse above and you complete a roll as you burst through the treetops.

Once above the forest, you fall back into line with the angel and the eagle. The angel smiles—knowing how much you enjoy your forest flights—as you glide up next to the eagle and stroke her outstretched wings. In the distance you see where the forest ends and a large meadow begins. This meadow is the land inherited by one of your friends. You swoop down to get a closer look and see if you can spot her.

Sure enough, she's out in her orchard, picking fruit. You descend even lower and she waves, always happy to see a friend. Flying overhead, you shout that you'll be back in a little while, then dart upward, just missing her roof.

A few more miles of hills and valleys pass beneath you until you see another friend's land. This friend has spotted you first, however, and he's already taking off toward you. He meets you on your way down, and you fly side by side for a while. You invite him to come to your place for a visit and he takes you up on the offer as he glances up at the angel and eagle overhead.

Nearing your own land, you see several angels flying westward and you exchange waves as you intersect their trail. You wonder if they are headed to the throne of God. Just the thought of that place excites you, and you suggest to your two companions that the three of you go there after showing the eagle her trees. They readily agree as you see your home in the horizon.

You ask the others to lead the eagle to the new trees you point out, and then you angle off toward your house. You have something for your two friends that you think they will appreciate. Hovering over your balcony, you slowly settle upon its husky rail. You hop down and open the large doors that lead into your upper room. Like your main room in the city, it isn't called a "bedroom," for in this land you never sleep, nor grow weary. But this room is still a favorite spot to come and relax, taking a break from the endless activities. On one of your shelves you grab two glowing, blue stones that you found on your last expedition, and head back out the doors.

The eagle seems to have already taken to your new trees, as she sits perched atop one of their branches. She calls out in that famous eagle cry, and you know she likes what she has found. Your two friends have landed and are standing beneath the new trees. You glide over and gently touch down beside them.

Eagerly you hand your friends the gifts and they respond with surprised delight. Service is what this universe is all about. You love giving gifts to your friends, for it really is more fun to give than to receive. The angels have told you that they were amazed at how slow humans were to grasp this truth in the old earth. The unconverted mind indeed could not grasp it.

As your friends express their gratitude, you suggest that the three of you go and thank the Creator of the stones right now. After all, He made the stones, all you did was find them. Your friends agree and the three of you take off toward Holy City. It is now time for your favorite flight of all: the flight that leads to the throne of your Father.

"For as the new heavens and the new earth, which I will make, shall remain before me, saith the Lord, so shall your seed and your name remain. And it shall come to pass, that from one new moon to another, and from one sabbath to another, shall all flesh come to worship before me, saith the Lord." —Isaiah 66:22, 23

There is something special about getting together with friends and loved ones. Humans were created to take pleasure in fellowship, and God Himself declared that it wasn't good for a person to be alone (see Genesis 2:18). We enjoy not only small gatherings, but larger get-togethers like family reunions, school reunions, church functions, and even notable public events. But what would it be like if such a gathering was filled with hundreds of your best friends? Imagine if everyone you met there was a person you simply cherished—someone you loved being around and with whom you had great memories. Now imagine if it wasn't hundreds of friends, but rather thousands, yea *millions*.

God promises us that in the new earth all flesh will come and worship before Him. Can you imagine the scene? All flesh—all people, all of the redeemed—will come together in one place and worship the Lord. What a scene that will be. "After this I beheld, and, lo, a great multitude which no man could number, of all nations, and kindreds, and people, and tongues, stood before the throne, and before the Lamb, clothed with white robes and palms in their hands" (Revelation 7:9).

From one new moon to another and from one Sabbath to another every single one of those who have been redeemed by the blood of the Lamb will gather together and worship their King. Not one will be absent. Everyone from Adam to those alive at the Second Coming will be present in that congregation. The new "moon" spoken of here is simply the Hebrew term *chôdesh*, which means "month." In other words, from one Sabbath to the next, month after month, for as long as God's throne exists, all flesh will come to worship Him. And as these weekly gatherings continue, your number of friends will multiply, for you will be meeting more people all the time. Your love for the Lord will also increase, so each meeting will be more eagerly anticipated.

The Sabbath is the day that will host these great gatherings. It is an eternal sign to remind all humanity of the One who made planet earth. Way back at the beginning of our world's history, God decided to end His week of creating in an interesting way:

"And on the seventh day God ended his work which he had made; and rested on the seventh day from all his work which he had made" (Genesis 2:2).

God obviously doesn't need physical rest like you and I; He is omnipotent. He simply laid aside the act of working and took in all that He had made, which He declared to be "good." Sin had not yet entered into the human family, and God was pleased with every perfect thing that had just come forth from His hand. Adam and Eve no doubt witnessed God enjoying this rest, for they were able to hold face to face communion with Him on a daily basis. This rest day came the day after they had been created, so they no doubt had lots of questions for the Lord at that time.

They then watched God do something quite extraordinary to that day. He actually made it holy.

"And God blessed the seventh day, and sanctified it: because that in it he had rested from all his work which God created and made," "For in six days the Lord made heaven and earth, the sea, and all that in them is, and rested the seventh day: wherefore the Lord blessed the sabbath day, and hallowed it" (Genesis 2:3; Exodus 20:11).

The day was sanctified, blessed, and hallowed by God Himself because He had rested on that day. It will forever point back to the genesis of our planet and race. In a world which is being bombarded by theories of big bangs and apes, it is refreshing to know that there is indeed a loving God who in fact created us all.

In the new earth, the redeemed will forever remember and honor this fact by their attendance at these global gatherings.

"All the ends of the world shall remember and turn unto the Lord: and all the kindreds of the nations shall worship before thee" (Psalm 22:27).

And what a worship time it will be! There we will not have to listen to the truth through a mere human instrument; the Lord Himself will "teach us of his ways" (Isaiah 2:2,3). The mysteries and depths of the love involved in the Plan of Salvation will continually be more clearly revealed. To be in that multitude is worth more than all of the temporal things of this world combined! May the Lord help us to decide this day that by His grace we will give ourselves 100% to Him and ultimately praise His name forever upon the Mount of Congregation.

❖ ❖ ❖

The Sabbath has come. It is time to go forth to the great meeting at the throne of God. You look forward to this day every week, and today is no exception. Last week's meeting was even better than the week before, which was better than the week before that. The meetings are continually becoming more of a blessing to you, because as the mysteries of God's infinite love unfold before you, the new information only enhances what you previously knew. Thus it has been for the last 10,000 years of your life and thus it will always be.

You feel like walking to the great assembly today, and you look forward to friends you'll inevitably meet along the journey. Before descending your front stairs, you stop to take in the beauty of God's creation. You never tire of looking at the trees and flowers as they sway in the gentle breeze. Thousands of bright orange butterflies flutter across the meadow from flower to flower. Recently there were vivid blue ones, and before that the yellow ones dotted the land. Typically a variety of them come together to decorate the scene with a medley of colors. You walk down the stairs as a fragrant breeze flows around you. The sky's canvass above is splashed with a royal blue. Your mind races as you think about today's meeting with the King.

A curious deer approaches you, and you reach out to touch her head. The fur is soft and smooth. You stroke her neck a few times before she wanders over to the pond for a drink. Continuing down the path in front of your home, you think about all of the others who are making this same journey right now. You break forth into a joyful song as you contemplate this world in which you live.

You travel several miles before entering your neighbor's land. In the distance, you see that he is just leaving his home, but he spots you, and gestures for you to come over to where he is standing. You notice that he's looking up at something in a tree and you break into a trot as your curiosity grows. He smiles as you approach and points toward the small tree. At first you see nothing, but then you realize that among the branches sits a furry koala bear, nearly camouflaged by the foliage. Your friend explains that he's never seen this bear before. With no cares of frightening him, the two of you approach the tree and reach up to pet his soft fur. Your neighbor offers him an apple which he promptly takes, as your friend promises to bring more food when he returns from the New Jerusalem. You bid the bear farewell and continue your journey to the Holy City.

Eventually you reach another home, but its occupant has already left. At the next house, however, a dear friend of yours is still inside and just ready to leave. She answers the door and is delighted to see you. She says she would love to join you, and the three of you proceed down the front steps and through her rose garden. Next you cross a stone bridge over a large river, and then head off into the woods toward the New Jerusalem.

This forest is nothing like the woods of old earth. Not dark and gloomy, but rather light and cheerful. You walk along the edge of a creek that leads to a magnificent waterfall. Your guide begins singing a song as you see the waterfall in the distance through the trees. She has picked a song which was penned by king David long ago: "This is the day which the Lord hath made; we will rejoice and be glad in it!" (Psalm 118:24). The song epitomizes your feelings: the Sabbath truly is a wonderful blessing.

Soon all three of you are glorifying God in perfect harmony. Praises to God are not only pleasing to the ear, but they raise your joy to an even higher plane. You and your friends have walked this trail a thousand times on the way to see the King, and each time you learn something new about this place. The trail winds around behind the waterfall, and you continue your song as the mist gently settles on your skin. The song takes on a unique tone as it fills the chamber behind the waterfall. You exit the other side and your eye catches the dazzling rainbow that appears in the mist from the falls. Below the rainbow thousands of bright red, yellow, and blue fish fill the crystal pool. The light that covers the planet sparkles off the top of the water and shimmers against the rocks behind you.

You ultimately exit the woods where you get your first glimpse of the distant Holy City. Although still hundreds of miles away, its towering jasper walls shine forth above the remote foothills. With your enhanced faculties and ability to fly, you can run, think, or soar to any point on the earth within a few minutes. A journey that would have taken months in the old earth is now accomplished during an enjoyable outing with your friends.

Just outside the woods you are joined by yet another friend who almost always waits for you in the exact same spot. He sits on the grass, leaning against a giant oak tree flanked by several azalea bushes. He remains seated and smiles as he joins in at the very close of your song. As the three of you approach him, the chorus ends and he rises to greet you. He says he can't wait to hear what Christ has to say this week, and the four of you begin to discuss all of the amazing things you learned last week from the great Teacher.

Your journey over the various landscapes swells your little group from four to several dozen before you know it. Every one of these people is dear to you and the chemistry between all is strong. No one will ever be an outsider in this land.

Upon reaching the rolling foothills that lead to the east wall of the city, you see that numerous groups like yours are merging and forming larger and larger groups. These gorgeous hills are covered with roses and lilies which, as perfect as they are, seem to get even brighter and more beautiful the closer you get to your glorious destination. More hymns are sung and as the multitude grows you begin to see a few people whose faces aren't familiar to you. Such people are becoming less and less common as you are constantly making new friends, especially at these weekly gatherings.

The features of the New Jerusalem are becoming more defined as you ascend its closest hills. It fills you with just as much awe now as it did the first time you saw it thousands of years ago. The most exciting part is the fact that God Himself sits within those walls. The Father and Son reside at the top of this enormous metropolis.

The growing mass of people seems to be electrified by the fabulous view as scores of them anxiously break into a trot. Several burst out in praise with a song about the city and its Builder, and soon thousands upon thousands of voices have united in harmonious exaltation. The light from the throne that bathes the earth simply floods these foothills, and you quickly join those who run toward its Source. The great hill is getting steeper as you near the jasper walls, but you don't grow weary in this land. As you make your way up the tremendous incline, you stop for a moment and turn to look around you. The bottom of the hill is covered with advancing worshippers clothed in white. What a sight! Up ahead and above you are more of God's children and beyond them the city's great eastern wall which stretches for hundreds of miles to the north and south, as well as into the sky. All around you, as far as the eye can see, people are ascending the great slope. The hill is just loaded with countless souls, all seeking the same goal: to be with their Savior. He whom they so persistently sought in the old earth they now have the privilege of seeking here. And just as the Lord promised, those who seek, indeed find.

Some people wait for companions beneath the branches of the hillside trees. You recognize one woman who smiles as you pass by. You met her a few hundred years ago at one of these assemblies and she has been a dear friend ever since. Far ahead up the steep incline you see a man leaving one of the trees and walking down a few steps to greet his friend. They embrace and turn to start their climb again. The city wall towers up ahead and the enormous pearl gate invites all to share the glories within. Looking up the side of the wall from here has always been one of your favorite sights for some reason. That glimmering surface rising straight up from the earth as far as the eye can see; that immense center gate ablaze in pearly white; the glory from the very throne of God illuminating the entire massive structure; everything about this view just seems to captivate your senses.

The center gate on this eastern wall bears Reuben's name and it, like the other 11, is attended by a large angel who shines like the sun. He welcomes you with a loving smile as you pass through the ever-open portal.

Inside the city, you and three of your friends walk along main street which is bustling with people. All are heading toward their Father's throne to worship Him as a united family. All retrieve their harps from their homes within these walls. All faces shine even brighter now as they near the Source and Origin of all glory.

You and your friends are climbing a great, golden staircase. The River of Life passes just beneath you as it flows from a giant waterfall to the west. Your soul feels perfectly at home here, and you and one of your closest relatives have decided that after the worship time, the two of you will stop by your home here and have a nice visit.

Now you enter the Great Congregation. The light in this place, shining from the throne of God and reflecting off the robes and faces of the redeemed, is awe-inspiring. You are now standing at the very brightest spot in the entire universe. The One who upholds the worlds and controls the movement of the tiniest particles of the atom sits before you on that massive throne. The One who can create living personalities from nothingness by the power of His voice, you are now seeing face to face. The Son of God and His Father both sit on the throne and all their children now bow in reverence and adoration.

Upon rising, you and the others quickly find your seats as a cherubim orchestra begins performing its most recent masterpiece. Worship cannot start until all are present, and the Lord knows if even one saint is missing; each soul is priceless to His heart. But attendance isn't a problem here, for all His children long to be in His presence. Just as they loved both God and fellowship with one another in old earth, so they love it here.

As the great multitude grows, so does anticipation. The Lord scans the sea of faces and it is clear by His expression that His joy is complete.

Finally the last of the redeemed come in and find their places. A hush settles over the multitude, and though you've experienced this many times before, you still marvel that so many beings can be so utterly silent. The Lord then motions to the orchestra to play a particular song that starts the meeting. The orchestra begins and the music floods every inch of that great city, resonating out into the farthest reaches of the universe. Each musician in the great multitude knows exactly where to join in and they do so at their designated time. You never realized on the old earth just how wonderful singing really could be. It lifts your spirits like few things can.

Now the Lord does something that no one on old earth ever witnessed. The Creator of music actually begins to sing to you! The prophet Zephaniah is there and he sees the words of his own prophecy fulfilled to a tee: "He will joy over thee with singing" (Zephaniah 3:17). In that song lies the power of creation itself, for His very words formed the earth. His song surpasses anything human or angel can produce. The arrangement of melody and lyrics has an invigorating effect upon the soul that can be found nowhere else. Hearing Daddy sing makes up for all of the trials on earth. For you this is indeed "heaven."

The song ends and the Lord begins to speak to the assembly. He bestows many blessings on you and expounds upon things that had challenged even the most advanced minds. Every word breathes life into the soul. Everything about your Father is admirable to you. His kingly features are beyond handsome. His voice, sweeter than the richest music.

You glory in His presence and bask in His light. Never in the old earth could you possibly imagine that your greatest pastime amidst the limitless possibilities of the universe would be simply dwelling in the presence of God. To the unconverted it always sounded so boring. The carnal mind could never grasp the truth, for spiritual things are spiritually discerned. But by the grace of the Holy Spirit you know the truth. You know that you are where you are because Jesus gave all for you and asked you simply to believe and surrender. The words of God continue to fill your soul and you never want to leave this place. Praise be His holy name!

"Through faith we understand that the worlds were framed by the word of God" —Hebrews 11:3

"The works of the Lord are great, sought out of all them that have pleasure therein." —Psalm 111:2

For thousands of years people have enjoyed visiting distant lands. Not just to see the various landscapes and buildings, but often to absorb the rich details of the local culture.

If you were to win a free trip to Paris you wouldn't just tour the Eiffel Tower and then leave. You might want to explore the many historic landmarks. Or maybe you'd prefer shopping in some of the stores and sidewalk shops. You'd probably seek out a restaurant that captures the "flavor" of Paris. You'd even buy a memento or two to remind you of the trip.

Whether it's Paris, Moscow, Hong Kong, Tahiti, Martha's Vineyard, or even places like the quaint little tourist traps along historic Route 66, we humans like to check out all we can about any place we find fascinating. But even the most exotic destinations fall short of what God has in store for us.

At this point we should get one thing perfectly straight: there is no text in the Bible that says "And ye shall visit other worlds." Such a belief obviously shouldn't be listed among the basic, fundamental doctrines of Christianity. The Bible does not specifically say that there is life on other planets, although it confirms the fact that there is life outside of this world—angels traveling to and from heaven for one thing. Before we proceed with this chapter, I'd like to clarify that I do *not* believe in aliens or extraterrestrial creatures as they are presented by Hollywood. Such grotesque, villainous beings are not in harmony with Scripture. They, in fact, cast shadows of doubt upon the Bible and the mission of Christ in coming to this world. These creatures, without exception, seem to have no knowledge of a Savior named Jesus, who the Bible says created all things (see John 1:3; Colossians 1:16,17; Hebrews 11:3).

Most likely, it is to prevent just such inevitable wild speculations that the Bible remains somewhat vague on this subject (just look at all of the sensational theories that have developed about the Antichrist and the Mark of the Beast!).

Outside of our world, all creatures under heaven worship and adore the Father, Son, and Holy Spirit. They do not spy on humans from spaceships nor devise plans to take over the earth with their superior technology. Cherubim (Genesis 3:24), Seraphim (Isaiah 6:2), and other heavenly hosts all support God in His plan to save this world. The exception to this, of course, being Satan and the evil angels, who are spirits and not spaceship pilots (although many believe these demons are behind some of the paranormal incidents around the world). These are not beings from other planets; they are fallen angels who once lived in heaven itself (see Revelation 12:7-9; Luke 10:18).

The issue of whether or not there is intelligent life on other worlds has been debated among Christians for generations. Some pastors insist that there is, while others are convinced that it just cannot be. In this book we will consider the possibility of intelligent, heavenly beings existing on planets, perhaps on the other side of heaven. Remember that with God all things are possible.

So if the Bible—while not ruling out the possibility—doesn't specifically say that there *is* life on other planets, why talk about it? Well, let's do a little math here. Scientists have discovered over 200 billion suns in the Milky Way galaxy. Our own sun has nine planets circling it. Now considering that some suns probably have more than nine planets while others have less, let's just say that nine is pretty much average. If this were so, then there are around 1 trillion, 800 billion planets in our galaxy. But let's cut this down to an unrealistically conservative estimate and see what we come up with. Even if there were only one planet for every 200 suns, there would still be *over one billion planets* in this galaxy alone.

But how many *galaxies* are there? Well, four can be seen from earth with the naked eye. Ours, of course; and then there is the Andromeda Galaxy (a.k.a. Andromeda Nebula: 2.2 million light years away), visible from the northern hemisphere. Stargazers in the southern hemisphere can see two others: the Small and Large Megallanic Clouds (200,000 light years away). These three other galaxies would of course multiply the potential number of planets significantly. But these are just the galaxies visible to the naked eye.

With the aid of powerful telescopes, astronomers have discovered and named a multitude of galaxies, declaring that there are at least *50 billion of them out there.* Remember that ours alone has probably over a trillion planets within its borders. The math at this point becomes, pardon the word—astronomical. Add to that the fact that these are just the galaxies of which we are aware. What else is out there? This universe is simply loaded with planets, all created by God. With that in mind, consider the following words:

"For thus saith the Lord that created the heavens; God himself that formed the earth and made it; he hath established it, he created it not in vain, **he formed it to be inhabited**" (Isaiah 45:18).

Then we are told in Hebrews 11:3 and 1:1,2 that "the **worlds were framed** by the word of God," and "God...hath in these last days spoken unto us by his Son, whom he hath appointed heir of all things, by whom he also **made the worlds**."

God does not form worlds in vain; He creates them to be inhabited. In His foresight He knew that fallen man would one day reach the surface of the other eight planets in our solar system. He therefore left them barren, confining the destructive and polluting influence of sin to souls on planet earth alone. But in the great galaxies beyond, the worlds serve a purpose. It would seem a bit out of character for God to tell us when we get to heaven, "Yes, I created trillions of planets out there, but there is nothing on any of them. They are just taking up space." Can you imagine exploring the outer reaches of God's universe with nothing but dead planets to see?

In Job 38:4-7 we are told that at the completion of earth's creation "the morning stars sang together, and all the sons of God shouted for joy." Angels are sometimes referred to as "stars" in the Bible (see Revelation 12:3,4,9). But who are the "sons of God"? We know that Jesus is the one, true Son of God, so that phrase cannot be taken to mean others equal to Him.

Scripture tells us that anyone who is born again and created anew in Christ has become a "son of God" (see John 3:3,6; 1 John 3:1,2; Genesis 6:1-4). But more specifically, the Bible refers to Adam as "the son of God" in Luke 3:38. Adam was given dominion over planet Earth and would have retained that position had he not fallen into transgression (see Genesis 1:26; 1 Corinthians 15:22). This act brought death, and thus prevented him from being present at a great cosmic meeting when the "sons of God came to present themselves before the Lord" (Job 1:6). He, as the head of planet Earth, the "son of God" representing our world, left a vacancy at this meeting. But the vacancy was quickly filled by another who had no invitation.

"...and Satan came also among them. And the Lord said unto Satan, Whence comest thou? Then Satan answered the Lord, and said, From going to and fro in the earth, and from walking up and down in it" (verses 6, 7).

God knew full well where Satan had been, but this was asked for the sake of the others in the assembly. Not from heaven, nor from the other worlds did he come, but from the one fallen planet called Earth: the very planet for which God's beloved Son was to die. Christ's parable of the one lost sheep among the hundred signifies, in one sense, the sole dark spot—our planet—among the innumerable worlds (see Matthew 18:12).

God loves variety. Each of these distant worlds probably has its own culture, with each city or village being unique as well. Imagine all of the free restaurants, historic landmarks and local "atmosphere" that these millions of places have to offer. They are just waiting for you to check them out.

And there is another reason universal tourism is probable. The Cross of Christ will be our science and our song for all eternity. Of all the countless beings in this universe, only those from planet Earth have experienced redemption by the blood of the Lamb. Jesus loves all of His created beings, of course. But He *died* for you; for you and the inhabitants of Earth alone did He die. As stated above, we are the one lost sheep the Good Shepherd went out to find and save. No other planet has required His death to save its inhabitants from sin. Yet it is not for our planet alone that such a gift was given. The lesson wrought out in the Plan of Salvation is a lesson for all of God's unfallen universe. They too needed to see beyond any shadow of a doubt that Satan's way was wrong and that God did indeed know best. They needed to witness the thoroughly selfless love that was manifested in the gift of the Son. One of our greatest joys in the new earth and in traveling to worlds afar will be telling the inhabitants of those planets what it was like to be saved from the Fall by the Son of God. The twofold activity of studying the Cross and sharing our testimony will bring us a deeper fulfillment than anything else in the next life. Shouldn't the same should be true in this life?

This chapter is not written to "prove" anything. It merely presents ideas for contemplation. I hope you are blessed by this brief, extremely limited view of some of the secrets of the universe which are "past finding out" (Job 9:10).

❖ ❖ ❖

You have been planning this trip for quite some time. It was arranged so that you and three of your friends could all travel together. With the infinite number of things to explore and do, it was necessary to plan ahead.

Two of your friends arrive at your country home together. You offer them each a tasty drink, produced from your own vineyard, and lead them up to your balcony as you wait for the third friend. At first you discuss a new lake that you have considered developing on your land, but inevitably the conversation turns to Jesus. Love for Him is the one thing that all inhabitants of the universe have in common; they never tire of talking about Him.

Finally the third friend arrives and your group is off. Although you have a list of worlds that you'd like to visit, you don't have to rush to get them all in. You can spend as much time as you want at each, for eternity lies always before you.

Eight wings quickly propel you into the blue expanse above. Such freedom you could only dream of in the old earth. You all shout and sing praises to God in perfect harmony as you leave the atmosphere behind and begin your trek through outer space. Your wings, like those of the angels, are capable of operating even outside the realm of the earthly atmosphere.

Lunch time is spent at your first stop, three galaxies away. This village is known for its delicious use of a famous food that grows only in this region of this particular world. All of your friends who have tasted it have declared for the past 30,000 years that if you go there "you've *gotta* try it!" You have found a delightful little café on the edge of town. The delicacy is brought to you and your taste buds are not disappointed. Words cannot describe the scrumptious flavor that fills your mouth. You complement the chef for the fabulous meal, and he promptly gives all the glory to God for creating and growing the food in the first place.

A quartet arrives at your table and delights you with beautiful songs about the local culture and their love for the Creator. The last song is the one that is synonymous with this place, the one visitors most look forward to hearing. Large, colorful birds add their sound to the music and soon you and your three friends are singing along as well. Joy fills the room as all stop eating for a moment to join in on that famous last line, always sung slowly and loudly for a grand finale effect. The final note is a high one, and all cheer and praise God as the song ends.

Although there is absolutely no charge for any of this, you have brought along some small gifts of gratitude. The chef gratefully receives them on your way out, and tells the four of you that he looks forward to seeing you again in the future. You have all made a new friend, and with perfect memories, if you were to return in 100 billion years, your friendship would still be as fresh as if you had never left the little café.

In the streets some of the locals are offering you various gifts from their village. Not because they want something in return, but because they are filled with the love of God, and enjoy nothing more than sharing what they have with tourists. You and your friends gladly accept these small gifts. In particular you notice one memento that you instantly realize would go perfectly in one of your rooms; you know just where to put it.

It is finally time to go and you are eager to get to your next stop: a world which has planned to hear the four of you speak about how Jesus changed your lives. You bid your farewells to the local villagers and again raise your wings for departure. A hymn of praise to the Lord wafts up from the streets of this place as you ascend into the skies. Although the sweet chorus fades the further you get from the town, you know your memories never will.

The inhabitants of the planet to which you are journeying have heard of your appointed time of arrival. News has spread throughout the population and they are eager to listen to you speak. The planet has a reddish hue from a distance, but as you approach and slow your flight speed, the scarlet seems to fade and the green of a lush landscape fills your vision. You have been given a specific place to land and the directions are perfect.

The roof of the designated resort is just below you as you and your friends spread your wings to ease your landing. This is a patio-type roof, complete with sidewalks, trees and a shimmering blue, fountain-fed pool. Thousands of people surround the base of the building as you gently touch down on its roof. These holy people are eager to hear your personal story of how Christ changed your life. They know the history of the great controversy between Christ and Satan, but they never tire of hearing personal testimonies from each descendant of the Eden couple.

Although you were nervous about public speaking in the old earth, you and your friends are perfectly at ease addressing this vast crowd before you. The Holy Spirit resides within you and He is inspiring you as you speak. You use no microphone or speakers, yet the multitude below can hear you perfectly.

It seems as though you have only begun to speak of His love and life-changing grace, when you realize that the equivalent of six Earth hours have passed. The joy and thrill of telling that story reconfirms the fact that time really does fly when you are having fun.

At this point you take questions from the audience. Answering each question brings you increased satisfaction and you are again filled with amazement that the sovereign King died for you! You pause as emotions of love and gratitude flood your soul. One of your friends then senses your emotional state and she steps up to embrace you lovingly. Christ's love has the same effect on all of you. You finish your answer and your friend then speaks for a while, radiant with joy as she tells her own story.

After all of your friends have given their testimonies, the people invite you on a tour of their ancient city. This place is known for its incredible architecture and you have been anxious to see it for yourselves. You have seen trillions of buildings on billions of planets, and yet each one is so unique and beautiful that you're always ready to see more. Your knowledge of architecture is constantly increasing and you plan to use this new knowledge in future ventures.

Soon you are walking across an enormous swinging bridge that connects the two tallest buildings on the planet. The building you approach is a thousand stories high and was constructed a million years before the creation of Earth, yet it looks brand new. Its arches and pillars give it a look unlike any of the skyscrapers in old earth. You've never seen thousand-story pillars before.

Your guide gladly takes you from building to building, explaining their ever-increasing knowledge of architecture. You visit the Ruby Manor, with its dazzling opaque red walls, the Giant Fire Dome, constructed of one massive sheet of fire, and an extraordinary structure actually made of compressed air. It is invisible, yet strong as steel.

One of the buildings near a tropical beach has what looks like a waterfall that flows out of all four walls near the top and splashes down over the ever-widening sides until it lands in a pool, bright as the sun, around the base of the structure.

Following your guide's lead, the four of you jump off the edge of the neighboring building and fly down to get a closer view of this pool. As you land, you realize that this is not a waterfall at all, but rather a diamond-fall.

You scoop up the precious gems in your hand. Although these jewels are commonplace in the New Jerusalem, you are still impressed with their beauty. A new crowd has gathered and they invite all of you to sit by the falls and enjoy a cool drink made fresh from the local fruit. For years they have enjoyed many of the songs you have written and now they wonder if they could hear a few firsthand. They ultimately hand your group some instruments which you gladly accept. With the roar of the diamond-fall in the background and the gorgeous beach before you, the four of you then start in on some of your older, familiar ballads of praise, followed by a few newer ones.

Several hours pass and you return the instruments to your appreciative hosts. As the crowd disperses, the sun begins to dip into the watery horizon, spilling its gold all across the gentle waves. This world has three moons and two of them are rising over the water, invading a golden orange sky.

With some of the locals sharing the discussion, you try to decide which place to see next. There's the Annual Global Parade at one particular world and the Ice Metropolis at another. One solar system is about to have a planet-alignment celebration, complete with shooting star displays. Someone suggests the moon of one planet that is famous for its incredible lightning shows. These grand spectacles are continually active on the moon's dark side. And then of course there's that quaint little village on another world that your aunt said had the most unique network of tree cabins she had ever seen.

Ultimately you agree that your next stop should be the Labyrinth: a world which has utilized the planet's insides by creating a vast maze of underground tunnels, rivers, stadiums and cities. These interconnecting passageways—with openings ranging from several miles across to only a few feet—criss-cross their way to the very core of the planet. Sheets of magnifying, reflective glass are positioned so that the light from their sun is actually channeled into the depths of the Labyrinth and back out the opposite side. You've been told that because of this, as it rotates, the shadowed side of it appears to be covered with scattered flames. There are also the famous scavenger hunts throughout the planet: a favorite activity among the tourists.

As you rise to leave, you turn to your guide and ask him if he would like to come and visit you sometime in the new earth. His eyes light up and he readily accepts the offer. You have added yet another precious soul to your ever-growing circle of friends.

Sharing a few final hugs with your new friends, you say your good-byes. The four of you then ascend into the atmosphere and fly off toward the sunset. You will surely visit your new friends again.

As you contemplate the cosmos, you are amazed by the endless variety of worlds that still await your exploration. It would clearly take an eternity to see all of the things this universe has to offer. But you and your friends aren't worried. After all, that's exactly how long you have.

"For the Lamb which is in the midst of the throne shall feed them, and shall lead them unto living waters" —Revelation 7:17

Have you ever wondered what it would have been like to live, and walk, and talk with Jesus as His disciples did? Jesus told them that it was beneficial for them that He go to the Father, because if He left them, He would send the Holy Spirit, and through the Spirit He could be with them constantly (see John 16:7; Matthew 28:20). Therefore we have access to Christ now, just as they did, according to Jesus Himself.

The Bible says of Enoch: "And Enoch walked with God" (Genesis 5:24). During his life on earth Enoch had developed such a close relationship with God that it is described as "walking" with Him. What does it mean to walk with Jesus when we can't even see Him?

"He that saith he abideth in him ought himself also to walk, even as he walked" (1 John 2:6).

To walk with Christ, then, is to abide in Him. How?

"If ye keep my commandments, ye shall abide in my love; even as I have kept my Father's commandments, and abide in his love" (John 15:10).

To abide in Him is to submit fully to His will and obey Him in His strength; it is to be crucified with Him. Our will is to be lost completely in His will, trusting that He always knows what is best for us, without exception. Christ calls us to live by "every word that proceedeth out of the mouth of God" (Matthew 4:4). This cannot be done in your own strength, but God promises that it is He that "worketh in you both to will and to do of his good pleasure" (Philippians 2:13).

Jesus has a great wish for His children which He expressed in the world's most famous prayer: "Thy will be done on earth, as it is in heaven" (Matthew 6:10). To have the Father's will done on earth in the lives of human beings as it is done in heaven by the holy angels, is the plan Christ has for all of us.

When it comes to the will and law of God, we are told "his commandments are not grievous" (1 John 5:3). In fact, James calls it "the perfect law of **liberty**" (James 1:25). And David declared, "I will walk at liberty: for I seek thy precepts," "Blessed are the undefiled in the way, who walk in the law of the Lord" (Psalm 119:45,1).

Walking with Christ means allowing Him to strengthen us to accept *all* of that "good, and acceptable, and perfect will of God" (Romans 12:2). When we find ourselves rationalizing away any portion of what the Word of God tells us, we can know that we are no longer walking with Jesus.

"Can two walk together, except they be agreed?" (Amos 3:3).

Blessed is the person who takes the leap of faith and begins to personally experience the freedom and joy that comes from submitting to the will of our Creator—no matter how crucifying it is at first to the selfish, carnal mind. The will of God is the only path to true happiness. When one is surrendered to the providence of God in all things, there comes a peace in knowing that nothing can touch you lest it be the will of your loving heavenly Father.

Jesus experienced this on the grandest scale in the Garden of Gethsemene. The Father's will said Go to the Cross. Christ's human nature said Let this cup pass from Me. But then the Savior added, "Nevertheless, not as I will, but as thou wilt," "if this cup may not pass away from me, except I drink it, thy will be done" (Matthew 26:39,42). Nothing on earth was more important to Jesus than the will of the Father. It is because of His decisiveness on this point that you and I even have the opportunity to talk of such things as heaven. Following Christ by making the Father's will our top priority is the one sure way to keep from falling into spiritual darkness.

"He that followeth me shall not walk in darkness, but shall have the light of life" (John 8:12).

Letting Christ into our hearts fully, with no reservations whatsoever, is the only way we can ever "have the mind of Christ" (1 Corinthians 2:16), and experience His continual submission to the perfect will of the Father.

May God grant us the wisdom to make that decision today, and may we always be listening for His voice in the Scriptures as it says to us, "This is the way, walk ye in it" (Isaiah 30:21). Those who make such a decision will, by the grace of God, keep their garments clean. And to such Christ has promised "they shall walk with me in white" (Revelation 3:4).

❖ ❖ ❖

It is your quiet time alone with Him. You look forward to this time more than anything else. Endless are the activities to occupy the mind and challenge the intellect. Infinite is the universe, just waiting to be explored. But these simple walks with Jesus appeal more to your emotions and intellect than any of those things ever could. Your friendship with Him runs deeper than any other relationship you have known.

As you walk together beside the River of Life, Jesus explains how He, the Father, and the Holy Spirit were as One from eternal ages past. The idea that this man walking beside you never had a beginning is too great for even your perfect, new mind to comprehend. As a created being, the only thing you can relate to is a starting point for everything. Even your guardian angel was spoken into existence thousands of years ago. The way Christ explains it makes more sense than any explanation you have ever heard, and with each of these encounters the concept seems to be getting clearer. He knows exactly how much to reveal at each particular stage of your increasing mental development. His patient smile exhibits the constant and deep love that He feels for only you. Although He loves all of the redeemed equally, each one has a special place in His heart that only they can fill.

As you descend a marble staircase that leads to a bridge, the conversation turns to the Plan of Salvation. The Savior reveals different aspects of how the Great Plan was devised. The Trinity did not intend for the human race to fall into sin, but they foresaw it, and met the emergency with an agreement. The moment the guilty couple was to face the penalty of death, the Son would step in and shield them from the wages of their transgression.

At the bottom of the stairs you ask Jesus why the law could not have simply been changed so that the wages of sin were not death, but rather a lesser punishment to teach the guilty pair a lesson and simultaneously spare the Savior's life. Christ smiles and explains that the Word that goes forth from the mouth of the Trinity cannot be changed (see Psalm 89:34; 119:89; Micah 3:6; Isaiah 40:8). If it could, then God would cease to be God, for His Word would lose its power (see Isaiah 55:11). It would then appear as though God did not know the future in that particular case, and had to change His mind to cover for this oversight. Rather than let the unchangeable penalty fall upon the guilty race, Jesus chose to take their place. The requirements of the law were holy, just, and good (Romans 7:12), and only the life of One who was equally holy could be adequate as a substitute.

You stop at the base of the glistening bridge that spans the River of Life. That giant expanse of crystal clear water flows peacefully before you. Jesus leads you down to the water's edge, and invites you to partake once again of the refreshing, cool liquid that you have enjoyed so many times before. He is fulfilling Revelation 7:17 and giving to you the living water. This river flows directly from the throne of God, the Source of all life. You have experienced a wide variety of delicious foods and beverages since coming to this place, but none seem to refresh you quite like the water from this river.

As you partake of the water, your mind returns to the great Sacrifice that made this drink possible. The thought reemerges that your Friend didn't just step in to save Adam and Eve at the Fall, but to save you personally. He loves you so much, He would have done the same thing if you were the only one who had ever sinned! Sometimes in the old earth it was hard to believe that He could love you on such an intimate level. It seemed at times that His sacrifice was an impersonal event that happened two thousand years ago, and doubts were occasionally creeping into your mind as to just where you fit into His plan. Now as you look into His face, radiant with benevolence and love, you realize just how unfounded were your doubts. The glorious habitation of the human race will for all eternity be a testimony of just how much He cared for you. But the greatest testimony, and the Savior's greatest glory are the everlasting nail prints in His hands and feet, and the spear mark in His side. It is in perfect harmony with His character to have the only trace of the one rebellious planet's sinful history, be scars upon Himself.

You fall upon the Savior's breast and hold Him tightly. On the old earth you were never known for your emotional displays, but in His presence you just cannot help yourself. John 3:16, the world's most famous text, is a living reality this very moment. The Redeemer leads you onto the bridge and the two of you proceed across the River of Life. You have lots of other questions for Him, that only He can answer. The King of kings and Lord of lords, the Savior and Redeemer of mankind, has given you His personal attention. You cherish the thought as you watch the crystal waters flow peacefully beneath you. Oh, how you love these walks.

"For, behold, the day cometh, that shall burn as an oven; and all the proud, yea, and all that do wickedly, shall be stubble: and the day that cometh shall burn them up, saith the Lord of hosts, that it shall leave them neither root nor branch." —Malachi 4:1

When discussing the eternal realities of heaven and the new earth, the question eventually arises: What about those who will be lost? Where will they be and what will they be doing throughout the billions of millennia?

Many Christians are confused about the fate of the wicked. Some believe that the wicked will be burned up like stubble, leaving neither root nor branch, while others teach that the suffering and torment will go on in some dark corner of the universe throughout the ceaseless ages. Without a doubt this confusion stems from the wording of certain Bible texts. The subject of hell, like many subjects in the Bible, involves Scriptures that on the surface seem to contradict each other. Before we look at these particular texts, it would do us well to consider how God Himself is affected by the act of punishing the lost.

"Have I any pleasure at all that the wicked should die? saith the Lord God: and not that he should return from his ways, and live?" "For I have no pleasure in the death of him that dieth, saith the Lord God: wherefore turn yourselves, and live ye" (Ezekiel 18:23,32).

And God describes His "wroth" "determined upon the whole earth" as His "strange work" and His "strange act" (Isaiah 28:21,22). It is strange and quite painful for the Life-giver to have to put an end to some of His own children. He hates the act; it wounds His heart. But does He inflict pain on His children for all eternity? That is what we need to know. Jesus said in John 17:3 that it was vital to our salvation that we "know" just who God is. Is the God we pray to every day the same God portrayed as an all-powerful One who will plunge His own creatures into agony without end?

First let's look at a few texts that support the belief in a punishment that does indeed end. In the 37th chapter of the Psalms we find four verses that shed some light on the subject:

"For yet a little while, and the wicked **shall not be**; yea, thou shalt diligently consider his place, and it shall not be," "But the wicked shall perish, and the enemies of the Lord shall be as the fat of lambs: they shall consume away; **into smoke shall they consume away**," "I have seen the wicked in great power, and spreading himself like a green bay tree. Yet he passed away, and, lo, he was not: yea, I sought him, but he could not be found" (Psalm 37:10,20,35,36).

In Isaiah 47:14 we read: "Behold they [the wicked] shall be **as stubble**; the fire shall burn them; they shall not deliver themselves from the power of the flame: there shall not be a coal to warm at, nor fire to sit before it." Here we see that they are so completely consumed that there won't even be a coal or fire left smoldering.

But when does the Bible say that this fire takes place? When do the wicked become like stubble and turn into smoke, leaving neither root nor branch, or a coal to warm at? The Bible makes it clear that the devil himself will be thrown into hell and burned in the lake of fire (see Revelation 20:10). He and his demonic evil spirits will suffer right along with the wicked humans. And yet what does the Bible say about these evil spirits? "And the angels which kept not their first estate, but left their own habitation, he [God] hath reserved in everlasting chains under darkness unto the judgment of the great day" (Jude 6; see also 2 Peter 2:4).

These angels are reserved until the judgment of the "great day," which is of course the end of the world. The Bible gives further evidence that the fire that destroys the wicked is yet future through a number of passages. First of all, consider the fact that "Our God is a consuming fire" (Hebrews 12:29). It is in the presence of God's holiness that the fire does its job. "As smoke is driven away, so drive them away: as wax melteth before the fire, so let the wicked perish **at the presence of God**" (Psalm 68:2). "[The wicked] shall be tormented with fire and brimstone

in the presence of the holy angels, and **in the presence of the Lamb**" (Revelation 14:10).

The clearest text in the Bible describing the destruction of the wicked is found in Revelation 20. This chapter describes the end of the "thousand years" (verse 7), often referred to by Christians as "the Millennium." At the end of the Millennium Satan rallies the wicked who "live not again until the thousand years were finished" (verse 5). The Bible describes these people as "the rest" who had no part in the "first resurrection" (verse 5), which occurred at the beginning of the Millennium (as described in Chapter One of this book). Now Satan leads this group whose number is "as the sand of the sea" against the New Jerusalem, that "beloved city." Then the Bible gives us that clear text mentioned above: "And fire came down from God out of heaven and devoured them" (verse 9). The language is quite clear here; it *devours* them.

"Let the sinners be **consumed out of the earth**, and let the wicked **be no more**" (Psalm 104:35).

"Wait on the Lord, and keep his way, and he shall exalt thee to inherit the land: when the wicked **are cut off**, thou shalt see it" (Psalm 37:34).

"And ye shall tread down the wicked; for **they shall be ashes** under the soles of your feet in the day that I shall do this, saith the Lord of hosts" (Malachi 4:3).

Wherein lies all the confusion then? In texts that use phrases like "everlasting punishment" (Matthew 25:46), "fire that never shall be quenched" (Mark 9:43), and "tormented day and night for ever and ever" (Revelation 20:10).

The punishment is indeed "everlasting." There is no hope of a resurrection *ever* for those who are lost and consumed by the fire. Notice the phrase uses the noun punishment (result) and not the verb punishing (action). This punishment is described as "the blackness of darkness forever" (Jude 13; see also 2 Peter 2:17).

So then, the punish*ing* is fire, as bright and hot as the sun, in the presence of the Lamb; the punish*ment* is the blackness of darkness forever: the same non-existence they had before being conceived by their parents. This is the "second death" (Revelation 20:14), the final death.

But what about the "fire that never shall be quenched"? The word "quench" means "to put out." No one will put this fire out. It will do its work of consumption and then *go* out, leaving neither root nor branch, only ashes. If you have ever stayed up late camping, you inevitably have been faced with the decision: "Should we just let the fire burn itself out, or should we quench it before we go to bed?" Only you can quench it; the fire can never quench itself.

The Bible itself gives another example of a fire that was not to be quenched. In Jeremiah 17:27 we read God's warning that if His people in Jerusalem disobeyed, then He would "kindle a fire in the gates thereof, and it shall devour the palaces of Jerusalem, and it shall not be quenched." This prophecy was fulfilled in 70 A.D., when Titus destroyed the city with a fire that the Jews could not quench. It destroyed the whole city, but is obviously not still burning today.

And finally, what about that daunting phrase "tormented day and night for ever and ever"? The Greek word rendered "ever" here is *aion*, which can literally be translated "an age." The same word is used in Christ's statement that the parabolic great harvest will be at the "end of this world"—the end of the *aion*, or age (see Matthew 13:39). The word can mean either a *specific time frame* or *forever*, depending on its usage in the text. So then, one may quickly ask, how are we to know which definition to use in this troubling text about the torment of the wicked? In light of all the other texts we have studied, the answer should be clear. The wicked will be burned until the end of an *aion*. The end of the present "age" is when fire covers the earth and this world is re-created before our eyes (see 2 Peter 3:10-13; Revelation 21:1,5). God does not reserve some remote spot on the new earth for all of the lost to fill the air with their shrieks of agony. The cities of Sodom and Gomorrha are "set forth as an example, suffering the vengeance of eternal fire" (Jude 7). According to the Bible these are an example for us as to what ultimately happens to the wicked. Are Sodom and Gomorrha still burning today from their "eternal fire"? The fire *did its job* and went out (see also 2 Peter 2:6).

The parable of the rich man and Lazarus (Luke 16:19-31) has also caused confusion, but Christ never intended for all of the symbolism to be taken literally (the dead going directly to Abraham's bosom; the saved being able to converse with the lost as they writhe in pain; merely a drop of water on the tongue requested by one whose entire body was blistering in the flames, etc.). Christ was not giving a discourse on hell, but rather teaching some very important lessons for both the Jews in His day and religious people today.

Think it through. We are talking about the very *character* of our Savior here. If God were to actually plunge His own lost children into unfathomable agony without end, He would break all world records for the most evil being that ever lived. The monstrous dictators that have come and gone in our world would look like merciful amateurs in comparison.

Many have stayed away from the Christian faith because of just such false representations of God. They cannot bring themselves to love an all-powerful being who feels He has a right to torture human beings for all eternity. And how can we blame them? The good news is that although punishment is indeed coming for the wicked, all suffering will finally come to an end. Our loving, tenderhearted God Himself would be living an eternal hell if He had to inflict or even be aware of such endless pain. Never again would His benevolent heart find happiness as He lived with the knowledge that multitudes were suffering with no hope of relief. Both the body and the soul will be consumed by the flames. The Bible is quite clear in regard to the end of the wicked:

"The **soul** that sinneth it shall **die**." —Ezekiel 18:20

"[God] is able to **destroy both soul and body** in hell."
—Matthew 10:28

"For the day of the Lord is near upon all the heathen: as thou hast done, it shall be done unto thee: thy reward shall return upon thine own head....and **they shall be as though they had not been**." —Obadiah 15,16

More and more Bible scholars and pastors of the various denominations are discovering and embracing the truth about the fate of the lost. Thank God He has given us the Bible so that we may see from His Word that such cruelty is out of harmony with His character. And thank God the following scenario is one that will fortunately never take place in the earth made new.

❖ ❖ ❖

You are on your way to see Jesus. Your heart thrills over the love and grace that He has shown you. You speed up your pace because you are eager to ask Him some questions about the eternal mysteries of Redemption. Studying His love and the miracle of the Plan of Salvation is the favorite subject of the ransomed, and you break into a run up the giant, golden staircase in joyful anticipation.

At the top of the ascent you enter the Great Throne Room where the Redeemer sits in all His glory beside the Father. You bow in adoration and then rise to converse with your best Friend. He tells you that He wants you to walk with Him as you speak. The King rises and steps down to meet you. His tall figure leads you out of the Throne Room and down the towering golden staircase. The view from the top of the stairs is breathtaking. You are many times higher than any skyscraper in the old earth, and yet you have no fear of heights whatsoever. You are in the presence of the Life-giver and nothing can harm you now.

As you descend the stairs Jesus tells you that He is going to oversee the Justice of His Righteousness. He warns you that this will not be a pretty sight, but reassures you that your own fate is eternally secure.

Walking together along the ground now, you begin to notice an awful stench. The smell is putrefying and gaining in strength, and you realize that Jesus is leading you to that Pit of Eternal Anguish. The wails and shrieks of a billion souls grow louder as you approach the giant chasm. The reek of burning human flesh stings the insides of your nostrils. Black smoke ascends from the pit, and you can see frantic movement within the molten brimstone below.

As you hold your nose and step up to the edge of the cliff, a relative of yours—a very close relative—recognizes you. She bellows out your name and begs you to dip your finger in some water and then put it on the tip of her tongue. Then she disappears beneath the surface of the flaming lake. You look to Jesus who seems saddened by all of this. You ask Him if your relative has suffered enough. After all, she has been in this torture chamber for several years now, and the punishment seems sufficient to you. But the Creator declares that no, there is never to be any rest for your loved one. A tear begins to form in the Savior's eyes as He scans the fiery horizon. He can never transport this torture chamber to a remote corner of the universe, for the wicked must be tormented in the presence of the Lamb, as His own Word declared. The heat is even beginning to warm your own skin a bit and you move back from the smoky edge.

As your relative comes back up to the surface, she releases yet another shriek of agony that pierces your very heart. You quickly divert your eyes as you hear your name called out once more.

You try again to convince the loving Savior that maybe it would be best to put this woman and these other poor souls out of their misery. But Jesus again shakes His head, declaring that the wages of sin is not death, but rather eternal suffering and ever-increasing torment.

Slowly you turn from the scene. You are no longer in the mood to ask Jesus your questions about the Cross, for these images have burned their impressions upon your mind.

Ultimately you find yourself contemplating this scene back at your comfortable estate with all its amenities. How can you ever enjoy this peace and quiet, or even fellowship with the Lord, when you know that your loved one is at that very moment suffering pain beyond your worst imagination?

Time passes and you now find yourself once more at the horrible chasm. Several people scream out to you for help before being sucked down by the white hot liquid. You hope that your loved one doesn't see you. Again you plead with Jesus to put these poor, suffering folks out of their misery and make them like they were before they were born: as if they had not been. After all, it has now been *two thousand years*, and not even the oldest human in this lake of fire lived long enough to warrant this kind of punishment. But alas, Jesus shakes His head and says that their punishment has only begun, and justice must be served; this is what these people deserve. You begin to wonder just how a created being like yourself acquired more love and mercy than the infinitely loving and merciful Creator. Suddenly you hear a gargling, screaming voice call out your name. Your relative has spotted you and she reaches out for help, arms dripping with flames. Again you turn to Jesus, but He reluctantly shakes His head No, before you can speak. Thoughts begin to creep into your mind about your Savior that you quickly dismiss for fear that they will grow.

Time has passed and you are again in your home contemplating just what you can do to save your poor loved one. What if you gave back all of the heavenly blessings Jesus bestowed upon you? What if you traded places with the lost woman? Perhaps you could pray for a thousand years, and at the end of the thousand years your prayers would be answered. The fate of the lost has begun to take over your mind, and nothing seems pleasurable anymore.

Ultimately you find yourself for a third time with Jesus at the edge of the monstrous, hideous pit. *200 million years* have now passed, and the shrieks and wails have only grown louder. Without even the hope of relief by losing consciousness, these poor souls have been suffering every second since you came into Paradise.

Your relative is still in the identical condition and as she shouts your name you wonder how in the world any being could withstand such agony for so long. Only God's power must be keeping the poor woman alive, for only God can give life. Now the Live-giver, however, is using His powers to prolong the suffering. He is keeping the consciousness alert so that the keen pain can never subside.

The heart of Jesus seems to be ripped right from Him. This place where all tears were to be wiped away now only creates and perpetuates the tears. You weep bitterly for these people and you wish more than anything in the universe that you were in charge and not God. If only you could somehow convince this Being that enough is enough! You fall on your knees, tears flowing down your cheeks, and tell Him that you can't stand any more. This is the closest you have ever come to speaking hastily to the Savior as you beg Him to put them out of their misery.

But once more the Sustainer of all life insists that justice has not been served. He starts to explain why He must keep them alive as you turn from Him and helplessly stare into the molten torture chamber. You aren't even listening, you are so overcome with pity for your fellow human beings. It now dawns on you that yes, you are indeed more merciful than this God who stands behind you. With no other choices you finally turn to Him and cry that if He will not put them out of their misery, then please, please, please, put you out of *yours!* You see that Jesus Himself is also miserable and will be for all eternity. You can no longer endure living in His new earth. To go on any longer would not be heaven for you, but rather a living hell. Although the flames do not engulf you, you realize that mentally you must share in the fate of the lost, and suffer without end.

❖ ❖ ❖

Reader, believe on the authority of God's Word that the scenario you just pictured will never, ever take place. Let us always remember that it is Satan who enjoys punishing and inflicting pain. Although justice will be served in the destruction of the wicked, never forget that "**He retaineth not his anger <u>for ever</u>, because he <u>delighteth</u> in mercy**" (Micah 7:18).

"Saying with a loud voice, Worthy is the Lamb that was slain to receive power, and riches, and wisdom, and strength, and honour, and glory, and blessing." —Revelation 5:12

"For I determined not to know any thing among you, save Jesus Christ, and him crucified." —1 Corinthians 2:2

What is it that makes the inheritance of the meek possible? What reveals the love of God more than anything else? What exhibits His perfect justice and hatred for sin most clearly? What is it that makes the cleansing from sin possible? And what is it that supplies us with power to overcome sin? The answer to all of these questions can be nothing else but the Cross of Christ. This is why Paul declared that he was determined to know nothing except Jesus and Him crucified. But do we naturally feel this way about the Cross? Does the unconverted person even see all that is involved in it?

"For the preaching of the cross is to them that perish foolishness; but unto us which are saved it is the power of God," "But the natural man receiveth not the things of the Spirit of God: for they are foolishness unto him: neither can he know them, because they are spiritually discerned" (1 Corinthians 1:18; 2:14).

The "natural man" is the person who has yet to be converted. Many are those who call themselves "Christian," but this title is no guarantee of conversion. After more than three years of training him, Jesus said to Peter, "When thou art converted, strengthen thy brethren" (Luke 22:32). Without true conversion the power of the Cross shrinks down into a dead theory or doctrine to learn once and look at again every Easter or so.

It would do us well to contemplate the life and death of Jesus every day of our lives: just to spend some thoughtful time allowing the Holy Spirit to make the Sacrifice real to us so that it is no longer "foolishness" or a lifeless doctrine. When we begin to do this, the Cross then becomes what it was meant to be: "the power of God."

And how is it the power of God to the converted soul? How can it give us victory over sin? The more the Holy Spirit impresses upon our minds the suffering our sins caused Jesus, the more anxious we will be to put those sins away, by the grace of God. We have all heard the Proverb "The fear of the Lord is the beginning of wisdom" (Proverbs 9:10), but what exactly is meant by "the fear of the Lord"? Part of it is a holy reverence for Him, but the Bible gives us another definition as well: "The fear of the Lord is to hate evil" (Proverbs 8:13). Nothing can make us hate evil so much as Calvary. Seeing our best Friend upon the Cross is the world's greatest antidote for a life diseased with sin. Until we allow the Holy Spirit to impress this great truth upon our minds, we will "continue in sin, that grace may abound" (something that "God forbid[s]"), and "crucify...the Son of God afresh, and put him to an open shame" (Romans 6:1; Hebrews 6:6).

But do we stay away from Jesus until we *feel* repentance for sin? Not at all. We must come to Jesus *for* this repentance just as surely as we need Him for pardon. Christ is described in the Bible as the One who is able to "give repentance to Israel, and forgiveness of sins" (Acts 5:31). Jesus gives us the ability to repent. It is a gift, there for the asking. We cannot change our own hearts, we cannot change our motives, but we can freely come to Him and ask Him to change them for us. Then He gives us the gift of repentance, followed by the forgiveness of sins.

And how does the Cross bring about the cleansing we so desperately need? By the precious blood of the Lamb that was shed.

"Forasmuch as ye know that ye were not redeemed with corruptible things, as silver and gold....But with the precious blood of Christ, as of a lamb without blemish and without spot," "and without shedding of blood there is no remission," but "it is not possible that the blood of bulls and of goats should take away sins" (1 Peter 1:18,19; Hebrews 9:22; 10:4)

His blood is the only substance in this universe capable of cleansing your record of sin. Why? Because "the life of the flesh is in the blood" (Leviticus 17:11). His very life must cover ours if we are to be found "faultless" (Jude 24) in the Judgment. "For we must all appear before the judgment seat of Christ" (2 Corinthians 5:10). As Jesus, our High Priest, administers His own blood on our sinful record, the record itself is changed to reflect His perfect record (see Hebrews, chapter 9 and Isaiah 1:18).

Had He failed even once while on this earth, and slipped into a sin of any kind, all hope for you and I would have vanished. There would have then been no blood found in the universe that could cover our sinful record. But praise be to God, Jesus did come off victorious, and He did set His face toward the Cross, no matter how strongly temptation beckoned Him to turn back. It is because of His death on the Cross that this blood is now available to be placed over our spotted record.

The Cross also reveals to us the immutability of God's law and His Word. Could the law have been changed, the Son of God need not have died. He could have simply remained at His Father's side on the throne of the universe and altered it to meet the emergency. But God's justice is equaled only by His mercy. Sin had to come to an end, and the definition of sin is "the transgression of the law" (1 John 3:4). Rather than let the punishment fall upon the transgressors of the law, Christ took our place. The real pain that Jesus suffered upon the Cross was not the nails piercing His hands and feet, but rather the sins of the world—your sins and mine—upon His very soul. This brought separation between Him and the Father, for sin always separates the soul from God (see Isaiah 59:2).

Justice and mercy met face to face in the Sacrifice on the Cross. "Mercy and truth are met together; righteousness and peace have kissed each other" (Psalm 85:10).

Just as clearly as the Cross reveals God's hatred for sin, it reveals His love for the sinner. When faced with the choice to let sinful mankind perish and retain His beloved Son at His side, or let His Son go down to the cold, dark world and experience the wrath of justice in place of mankind, He chose to send His Son. Is it not amazing that anyone could doubt such love? What more could He do? Often when we fall into sin, we conjure up pictures of a God who leans back in His throne with His mighty arms folded, reluctant to offer forgiveness. But this is all a carnal delusion. If God so loved the world that He gave His only Son to die in your stead, would He not be eager to pardon you after a fall? "Like a father pitieth his children, so the Lord pitieth them that fear him," "because he delighteth in mercy" (Psalm 103:13; Micah 7:18).

It is God who is there to lift you up when you fall. He is the One who reaches out His hand, pulls you out of the muck, and cleans you off. More patient than any earthly parent can be with a child is your Heavenly Father with you. The Cross reveals this more than anything else can.

And finally, how does the Cross give us access to heaven? First of all, it gives us power over death, the great barrier that sin erected over a rebellious planet.

"And if Christ be not raised, your faith is vain; ye are yet in your sins. Then they also which are fallen asleep in Christ are perished....For since by man came death, by man came also the resurrection of the dead. For as in Adam all die, even so in Christ shall all be made alive. But every man in his own order: Christ the firstfruits; afterward they that are Christ's at his coming....The last enemy that shall be destroyed is death" (1 Corinthians 15:17,18,22,23,26).

Christ's death on Calvary and His resurrection from the tomb revealed the power that unlocked the forces of death.

"Forasmuch then as the children are partakers of the flesh and blood, he also himself likewise took part of the same; that **through death** he might destroy him that had the power of death, that is, the devil" (Hebrews 2:14).

"I am he that liveth, and was dead; and, behold, I am alive for evermore, Amen; and have the keys of hell and of death" (Revelation 1:18).

Jesus' sinless life made Him the spotless and therefore worthy and acceptable Sacrifice on Calvary. By His resurrection (the result of His sinless life) He broke the curse of sin and made possible the resurrection of all who have believed on Him. It is because of His perfect Sacrifice, that at His Second Coming multitudes will declare as they come forth from their graves, "O death, where is thy sting? O grave, where is thy victory?" (1 Corinthians 15:55). Death will in that day be "swallowed up in victory" (verse 54)—the victory Christ gained on the Cross.

And there is another way that the Cross gives us access to heaven. The prophet John had a vision of the future, where a "great multitude" stood before the throne of God wearing white robes (Revelation 7:9). They still refer to Jesus as "the Lamb" (verse 10), signifying their association with His great Sacrifice. This great multitude is described as those who "have washed their robes, and made them white in the blood of the Lamb. Therefore they are before the throne of God" (verses 14,15). Notice the wording: *therefore* they are before the throne. Because they have washed their robes in Christ's blood, they not only receive forgiveness, not only receive empowerment, but they also gain access to the very throne of God in heaven. Had they not had this robe of Christ's righteousness—supplied by His cleansing blood—they would have been consumed with their sinful record in the presence of a Holy God, who indeed is a "consuming fire" (Hebrews 12:29).

"Blessed are they that do his commandments, that they may have right to the tree of life, and may enter in through the gates into the city" (Revelation 22:14).

To "do his commandments" is possible only through the blood of the Lamb shed on Calvary's Cross. "And they overcame him [the devil] by the blood of the Lamb" (Revelation 12:11). They did not overcome by their own efforts, in their own strength, with their own righteousness. It was by the blood of the Lamb that they were able to gain the victory and inherit eternal life in the New Jerusalem. The only way they were enabled to have His strength, was to die to self and the strength of self. "For ye are dead, and your life is hid with Christ in God" (Colossians 3:3). His blood not only covered their record of sin, but it empowered them to die to self and let Him live out His perfect life through them. Jesus, through His blood, obeys the Father in us.

Does the keeping of the commandments, then, save anybody? No, "For by grace are ye saved through faith; and that not of yourselves: it is the gift of God: Not of works, lest any man should boast" (Ephesians 2:8,9). The Commandments of God are the world's biggest and most accurate spiritual mirror. Not only do they protect us and provide a great blessing, but they reveal to us our true spiritual condition so that none deceive themselves into a false sense of security, while abiding not in Christ.

"But be ye doers of the word, and not hearers only, deceiving your own selves. For if any be a hearer of the word, and not a doer, he is like unto a man beholding his natural face in a glass [a mirror]: For he beholdeth himself, and goeth his way, and straightway forgetteth what manner of man he was. But whoso looketh into the perfect law of liberty, and continueth therein, he being not a forgetful hearer, but a doer of the work, this man shall be blessed in his deed" (James 1:22-25).

"And hereby do we know that we know him, if we keep his commandments. He that saith, I know him, and keepeth not his commandments, is a liar, and the truth is not in him," "By this we know that we love the children of God, when we love God, and keep his commandments. For this is the love of God, that we keep his commandments: and his commandments are not grievous," "And he that keepeth his commandments dwelleth in him, and he in him. And hereby we know that he abideth in us, by the Spirit which he hath given us." (1 John 2:3,4; 5:2,3; 3:24).

The law saves no one; Jesus saves. But since the fall of humanity, our carnal minds needed the law to be written down so that we would know the one, true path to follow, and to be aware of whether or not the Savior truly "abideth in us".

"Therefore by the deeds of the law there shall no flesh be justified in his sight: for by the law is the knowledge of sin," "Nay, I had not known sin, but by the law" (Romans 3:20; 7:7).

Without the law we would have no idea what sin is, and would not be aware of how much we need the Savior to forgive us and empower us. The law shows us what sin *is*. The Cross shows us what sin *did*. As we look upon these two we begin to grasp our true condition, and we run to the only One who can save us.

The Cross of Calvary brought to an end the whole sacrificial system that pointed ahead to Jesus, "nailing it to his cross" (Colossians 2:14). But thank God His eternal moral law, written with His own finger, endures forever (see Exodus 31:18; Psalm 111:7,8; Luke 16:17; Matthew 5:17-19). We are not left in darkness to be "carried about with every wind of doctrine" (Ephesians 4:14); we have God's unchanging Word as a guide: "a lamp unto my feet, and a light unto my path" (Psalm 119:105).

Reader, have you come to the Cross and dwelt at the foot of it? Have you witnessed the enormous price that was paid in your behalf? Perhaps you have never given your heart to Jesus and are learning about Him for the first time. Perhaps you have been a Christian for years, but had no idea of the limitless power of the Cross; you really *can* have victory over those inherited or cultivated sins. Maybe you are realizing for the first time what the definition of sin is—the transgression of God's law—and you want to come again to Jesus and have Him make things right. You might be one who once enjoyed sweet fellowship with the Lord, but have drifted far from Him on your prodigal journey; you know the path you should be on, but have deliberately chosen a course of sin and selfishness. Whatever your condition, no matter how dark your past, it is not too dark for the Savior to read and to cleanse. He waits for you even now as you read these words. He specializes in giving new starts: providing clean slates. He wants to free you from whatever is holding you back and show you who the *real* you is, the one He created you to be. Let nothing, nothing stand in your way of coming to the Savior now, just as you are, and letting Him give you the peace of total forgiveness, which surpasses all understanding.

The Cross was devised in a Master Plan by the Father and Son so that you could share in the pleasures of heaven and the joy of fellowship with your Creator. Do believe that in God's mind heaven will not be the same without you. In the Father's great house are many dwelling places, many "rooms" created for all of His children. One was designed especially for you. One has your name written over its door—a door just as real as the book you hold in your hand. It is no fantasy, no Christian daydream.

Do not wait until you feel "good enough" to come to the Cross, or you will never come. For the blood that it made available is the *only* thing that can ever take away your sins and transform you to reflect the selfless image of the Sacrifice Himself. Neither wait until you feel like you love Him. Always remember that both repentance and love, as well as a change of heart, come from God alone; they are not inherent traits of your soul. Romans 5:5 tells us that "the love of God is shed abroad in our hearts by the Holy Ghost which is given unto us." The ability to love the Lord is itself a gift from God. Give yourself to Jesus today, based upon the truths in His Word, and the repentance and love will come. The feelings that we so often rely upon as a guide will then take their true place, as the *result* of our decision, not the *deciding factor*.

As you come to the Lord in prayer, believe that God is always working; He never ceases (see Psalm 121:4). The repairs that need to be made upon your heart and soul will be underway at that very moment, though you may not feel it. The love of God will be shed abroad in your heart that very hour, though you sense it not. Trust in the Lord, and let Him do His work.

Then the Cross will begin to appear in its true power. The Great Sacrifice who hung upon it in your behalf will be seen in a whole new light. The truths which to your mind were either new, unfamiliar information or an old love which had waxed cold, will shine forth in an all new luster. Jesus Himself will cease to be a figure in history somewhere, whom you know so little about, and will become the "Sun of righteousness," rising in your heart "with healing in his wings" (Malachi 4:2). Then you will have the "peace that passeth all understanding" (Philippians 4:7), and Jesus will find a resting place in your heart. True life will finally begin and eternity will be yours, shared with the Man who was wounded for your transgressions and bruised for your iniquities, the Man by whose stripes you are healed.

❖ ❖ ❖

The world is watching. Inside the city of God stand the redeemed of all ages, clothed in white and shining "as the stars" (Daniel 12:3) as they reflect the glory of Christ. Outside the city, arrayed against it for battle, stand the rejectors of God's mercy: those who hardened their hearts against the tender promptings of the Holy Spirit. Their numbers are "as the sand of the sea" (Revelation 20:8,9). Sin is about to be eradicated from the universe. Those whose sins have not been placed upon the Cross and cleansed by the blood of the Lamb will share in the fate of their iniquity.

But before the end is to come "the earth shall be filled with the knowledge of the glory of the Lord, as the waters cover the sea" (Habakkuk 2:14). The glory of the Lord is His character, His perfect benevolence combined with His perfect hatred for sin. In order for the whole earth to be filled with a knowledge of such, they must first see it as it was most clearly manifested: in the Cross of Christ. The only way that "every tongue should confess that Jesus Christ is Lord" (Philippians 2:11), is if a view of the Great Sacrifice on Calvary is given.

While the scene speaks of judgment and guilt to those outside the city, it reveals love and grace to those inside. You, like the billions of others at this moment, cannot turn your eyes from the spectacle. There, above the City for all to see in panoramic view is the story of the great controversy between Christ and Satan. The closing scenes of the Savior's life are now presented before all.

In the darkness of the Garden of Gethsemene the weight of the sins of the world are pressing down upon Him. He knows where His path is rapidly leading, and He must decide now whether or not to go through with it amidst all of Satan's suggestions. He takes a few more labored steps and then falls to the ground in prayer. Beads of sweat mixed with blood are forming across His forehead, signifying the anguish of soul that is now His. Separation from the Father: never before experienced by this Man who has been one with the Father from eternal ages past. How easy would it be to now forsake the rebellious planet and return to the Father's side, retaining the throne and authority that are rightfully

His. How just it would be to let the guilty race pay the penalty which each one has brought upon himself. To turn back now and let the punishment fall upon mankind would be no travesty of equity, no miscarriage of justice. Rather, it would simply be the fair and deserved consequences, called for by the law of God: "The wages of sin is death" (Romans 6:23).

The Son pleads with the Father to find another way, if it be possible, to save the guilty race. He does not plead that perhaps the fallen world should perish so that He can avoid the Cross; His selfless interest in their salvation is unchanged. But the thought of separation from His eternal Father is horrifying. "If it be possible" to save the people He loves so much, in any other way, He asks that such a way be implemented. But no such way is found. The Son of God hears no alternate plan flowing down from the throne in heaven. The Word that goes forth from the mouth of God does not return to Him void, but accomplishes that which He purposes (Isaiah 55:11). It cannot be changed; no second option materializes. Sin must bring forth death (James 1:15).

Three times the Savior petitions the Father with the same prayer. Three times He hears no encouraging utterance that the cup of guilt can pass from Him. As you watch the scene you are fully aware that the decision is made for you. If *you* are to be saved, then the Redeemer must accept the cup and press on toward the penalty. His thoughts are on *you* as He makes up His mind. Although surrounded by billions, you are transfixed by the scene and aware of no one except your Savior, choosing to go forward and pay your price. To your grateful soul His choice now seems to have been made not for the sake of the multitudes, but rather for you personally. The magnitude of the thought that the King of the universe, the One through whom all things were made, gave Himself for *you*, is overwhelming. And yet the decision has been made. The Savior lifts Himself off the ground, willingly accepting the fact that there is but one course to follow if you are to be saved. Come what may, and whatever torment is brought to His own soul, you are worth it to Him. His face is set toward the Cross, and there is no turning back now.

In the distance Judas and the bloodthirsty crowd appear as Jesus rouses His sleeping disciples. Truly alone was He through His agonizing ordeal. The comfort of a friend, the joint prayers of His companions, would have lessened the pain and loneliness of His trying hour. But alas, "I have trodden the winepress alone, and of the people there was none with me" (Isaiah 63:3).

Upon seeing the approaching mob, several of the disciples brace themselves for the conflict. Ultimately, after being taken aback at first by the glory which surrounds the Savior and then fades, Judas steps forward and kisses the Son of Man. The one who for more than three years was in the presence of Love itself, now betrays the Savior for 30 pieces of silver. Oh, to what depths can the human mind sink when continuing down the path of sin!

Recognizing the kiss as their sign, the angry horde moves in to bind those precious hands that had healed so many. With one snap of His fingers the Lord could even now wipe out every man in that throng. But He knows that everything that happens henceforth is the Father's will, making possible your freedom from the penalty.

Seeing his Master's hands bound with so little resistance, Peter becomes indignant and draws his sword, lashing out at the high priest's servant and cutting off his ear. Consistent with His character, Jesus calmly releases His tightly bound hands and heals this malicious servant's ear. What must be done, must be done, and resistance is not in the Father's Plan. The Savior returns His hands to the bewildered throng as Peter and the others flee for their lives, forsaking their Lord. The crowd once more secures Jesus' hands and they hurry Him out of the garden like a common criminal.

You watch as Jesus is brought before the various authorities, each sending Him to yet another, none standing up to the injustice of it all. You cringe as you see numerous officers strike the Savior and treat Him with contempt. You witness Peter adamantly deny that he ever knew Jesus, and you know that by your own course of action you had done likewise on more than one occasion.

Ultimately Christ is brought for a second time to a Roman governor named Pilate. Pilate places Jesus and a criminal named Barabbas before a crowd which is then faced with a decision. He asks the Jews to choose which man he should release, which he should therefore condemn. This choice is one you had faced throughout your lifetime. In your daily walk with Christ, decisions arose which ultimately amounted to: Do you choose Jesus, or the world? There is no partnership between the two.

Now the decision of the crowd comes bellowing forth: "Barabbas!" And when asked what to do with the Savior? "Crucify Him!" Angels watch in amazement as the words ascend to heaven. The One who came to save the world is now being rejected by it. Christ indeed had to die, for this was the Plan of Salvation. He would inevitably be betrayed and sent to His death, for it was written that it should be so; "but woe unto that man by whom the Son of man is betrayed!" (Mark 14:21).

Although openly finding no fault in Him, Pilate allows Jesus to be chastised for the sake of pleasing the people. Already wearied from a sleepless night, and covered with wounds from spiteful hands, Jesus is publicly scourged and then taken into "the hall, called Praetorium." The whole band of Roman soldiers then gathers around Him and you watch as these infidels clothe Him in purple and place a horrid crown of thorns upon His tender head. Thorns, the very symbol of sin itself, placed upon the head of the sinless One, the spotless Lamb of God! Again the thought comes to you that with the raising of an eyebrow Jesus could lay His abusers into the dust. But for you and the prospect of your eternal happiness, the Redeemer accepts their cruel treatment. Now the soldiers begin to bow down sarcastically and salute Him, shouting, "Hail, King of the Jews!"

You then notice, unseen by His tormentors, several angels of God, faithfully recording every word and act. Little do these mockers realize that "God shall bring every work into judgment, with every secret thing, whether it be good, or whether it be evil," and "every idle word that men shall speak, they shall give account thereof in the day of judgment" (Ecclesiastes 12:14; Matthew 12:36).

The scene changes and now the dreadful sentence begins, much to the delight of the crowd: the Savior will finally be crucified. You watch as the cross which had been prepared for Barabbas is thrown upon His bruised and bleeding shoulders, and the Redeemer is forced to carry the burden. The penalty that had been prepared for you is borne instead by your great Substitute. He marches forward, determined to have fall upon Him a punishment which He cannot bear to watch you receive.

Along the dreadful path, many in the following crowd weep for the innocent Son of man. A large man named Simon is compelled to go and support the cross to its dark destiny, as the Savior's humanity, wearied from the beatings and a sleepless night, falls again beneath its weight.

Finally the train reaches a hill called Calvary. You watch as the cross is laid on the hard ground and Jesus is stretched out on top of it. His thoughts are on you. You are conscious that the prospect of your eternal salvation through what He is now doing is what keeps Him going. It was "for the joy that was set before him" of seeing you in His kingdom, that He "endured the cross" (Hebrews 12:2).

Large, cruel nails are brought to the scene and are driven through the willing hands of Jesus. "Behold, I have graven thee upon the palms of my hands" (Isaiah 49:16). As the nails pierce the skin and the blood is spilled, you are engraved there. You are worth *everything* in the world to Him, and forever will the scars on those palms testify to this fact. More nails piece His feet, and the magnitude of this moment with its eternal consequences washes over you. You witness the Savior being lifted up, the cross slamming roughly into its channel.

"And I, if I be lifted up from the earth, will draw all men unto me" (John 12:32).

This prophecy is now fulfilled in your sight as all men, all human beings, are drawn to the scene, captivated by the enormity of just how great that Sacrifice was. This "drawing" had already been working on the hearts of all, by the Holy Spirit, throughout their lives. Both the saved and the lost fully realize that nothing more could have been done to save them.

For hours He lingers on the cross. The crowd's mockery continues. Satan himself is there, pressing his sophistries upon the dying Savior's wearied mind. Here is temptation in the highest degree. If the deceiver can win here, the battle is over. The sun itself is stricken as its Creator's life is being drained, and darkness covers the cross for the space of about three hours. The separation is taking place. The separation that the impenitent sinner must face is transpiring in the soul of the Redeemer. This brings about a change in Him that He has never experienced. You know this because He cries out with a loud voice, "My God, My God, why hast Thou forsaken Me?" You are cognizant of the fact that Christ cannot now see through the portals of the tomb. He fears that the sin which He is now taking upon Himself is so offensive to the Father that the separation must be eternal. And yet He still remains true to His beloved cause. This is the course He is to follow, and although He feels forsaken, He trusts in the Father's Plan. He fully believes that His death will ultimately result in your redemption. And He knows that to escape now would most assuredly cost you your salvation. Thus, He endures the cross. Such a love has He for you!

As the Savior revives to a sense of physical suffering, He quietly says, "I thirst." His thirst is met with the prophetic sponge of vinegar, but even this act of sympathy angers the crowd. They had misinterpreted Christ's words "Eloi, Eloi, lama sabachthani" as a desperate cry for the prophet Elijah. Now they angrily declare with one voice, "Let be, let us see whether Elias will come to save him!" These pitiless, mocking words are the last ones the Savior hears before His life comes to an end.

The great multitude inside the city and the countless millions outside its walls all stand transfixed as the closing moments of the Savior's life pass before them. You now hear the three words that mean eternal victory to your soul. Jesus lifts His wounded, bleeding head toward the sky and declares in the voice of a Conqueror, "It is finished!" The words roll across the earth like peals of loudest thunder. And then the Redeemer adds, "Father, into Thy hands I commend My spirit!" Completing the work the Father gave Him to do, He bows His head upon His breast, breathes His last, and dies.

Satan is finally unmasked for who he really is: "the father of lies." All see the true character of the Enemy of souls in contrast to the perfect love of Christ. Truth is driven home to the conscience of every witness—the same truth which the Holy Spirit had been trying to impress upon humanity since the fall of Adam and Eve.

Although enraged with the outcome, and by no means in love with Jesus, the lost join the saved in fulfilling the prophecy of God.

"That at the name of Jesus every knee should bow, of things in heaven, and things in earth, and things under the earth; and that every tongue should confess that Jesus Christ is Lord, to the glory of God the Father" (Philippians 2:10,11).

The great multitude of the redeemed bow first, joined by the countless holy angels. Next the wicked outside the walls, the rejectors of God's persistent mercy, bend the knee. The fallen angels quickly follow suit in acknowledging the justice and fairness of Jesus. And finally Satan himself—the father of rebellion, the accuser of the brethren, and the enemy of souls—marches down to the gate of the Holy City, gets down on his knees, and declares that Jesus Christ is indeed Lord. In unison with the saved, the wicked declare "just and true are thy ways, thou King of saints" (Revelation 15:3). The truth has finally triumphed. The power of the Cross has been plainly revealed. Your best Friend Jesus sits on the throne of the Universe, acknowledged as "just and true" by all.

"That thou mightest be justified when thou speakest, and be clear when thou judgest" (Psalm 51:4).

Christ is indeed justified and cleared in the judgment of the wicked. The Cross demonstrates that there is nothing more He could have done. The eternal loss of the wicked was brought on by themselves in the face of overwhelming evidence of God's love. Their hardened, selfish, rationalizing hearts would find no joy in the peaceful New Jerusalem, where submission to God and loving obedience to His perfect will bring the utmost joy and pleasure. The words of truth that just came forth from their lips find no answering chord within their hearts. They know not the Savior.

The fulfillment of this prophecy is followed by a brief stillness, which covers the planet. For the first time in history every soul in the universe is thinking the same thing: God's ways are just. He always did have His children's best interest in mind with every instruction He ever gave. His government, His kingdom, is based on love. Satan's lies are forever exposed and sin will never raise its ugly head again. Their final acknowledgment of the truth is the last act of the wicked before they surround the city and are consumed by the fire. Sin and its adherents are about to be no more. The entire universe will once again be clean. From then on the prophecy of the Redeemer's exaltation will be fulfilled, not by lips compelled to speak the truth, but rather by those who love the truth and speak from the heart. For all eternity they will have the chance to praise, adore, and thank Him for all that He did on the Cross. They will sing with boundless love and gratitude, "Worthy is the Lamb that was slain!"

"But ye, brethren, are not in darkness, that that day should overtake you as a thief. Ye are all the children of light, and the children of the day: we are not of the night nor of darkness. Therefore let us not sleep, as do others; but let us watch and be sober." —1 Thessalonians 5:4-6

"It is time for thee, Lord, to work: for they have made void thy law." —Psalm 119:126

As we look at the world around us there can be no doubt that we are living in the last days. More and more people are wondering where society is headed as it seems to break down before our very eyes. Children are now taking the lives of other children. Crime in general is on the rise. Natural disasters are intensifying around the globe. An increasing number of nations are acquiring nuclear capabilities. Despite what the politicians promise, we know that things are only going to get worse. It is only by the grace of God Himself that we as a human race, even still exist. Long ago would we have extinguished ourselves had He not mercifully held back the process of self-destruction.

Nevertheless, the woes of our world continue to increase, and as a result, more and more people are starting to turn to the Word of God for answers. They remember hearing about strange disasters predicted in the book of Revelation. Their minds recall bits and pieces of sermons they heard as they flipped the channels on various Sunday mornings. They wonder, Is there any truth to these things? Whether longtime Christian or self-proclaimed atheist, many are beginning to take a second look, in fact a *deeper* look, at Bible prophecy.

Perhaps you are one who has studied prophecy and feel quite secure about the order of events that are to come upon this world. Maybe your pastor has done a Revelation Seminar, and you know all about who the Beast of Revelation 13 is, and can accurately identify the Mark of the Beast. Whether you feel yourself knowledgeable in this area or not, it would do us well to review some things that Scripture has been telling us for thousands of years—things that are soon to take place, probably in this generation.

The Bible offers a blessing for those who actually spend time studying the prophecies of Revelation. "Blessed is he that readeth, and they that hear the words of this prophecy, and keep those things which are written therein: for the time is at hand" (Revelation 1:3).

Perhaps in regard to Bible prophecy and last day events, you have told yourself, "When I begin to see these things happen, *then* I'll give my heart fully to the Lord." Sound familiar? This is a deception of the Evil One. The Bible says: "**To day** if ye will hear his voice, harden not your hearts" (Hebrews 3:15). Do you hear His voice today?

We will not go into detail as to the specifics of the Beast power, and if you are one who has no idea about such things, then please request the free Bible studies at the back of this book. Let's look now, however, at a few simple facts.

The book of Revelation tells us that a Beast power will deceive the people and cause them to make an "image to the beast" (Revelation 13:14,15). Deep inside, we all know that this is not talking about a giant statue in some metropolis of the world which we will all be forced to go and worship. Many Christian prophecy books are filled with James Bond type scenarios of a coming great villain who will have a giant tattoo machine which he uses to try and put a "666" on the foreheads of all 5+ billion of us. The Lord speaks plainly when He says, "Come now, and let us **reason** together" (Isaiah 1:18). God has given us enough common sense to know that these sensational speculations are as misguided as the Pharisees' views of the Messiah's role in the first Advent (and their errors led them to crucify Him!).

God calls on us in these last days to lay aside all the ideas and predictions of man, and turn to His Word as the only true and safe guide. "The grass withereth, the flower fadeth: but the word of our God shall stand forever" (Isaiah 40:8).

If we really want to know what is going to happen before Jesus returns, and how we can be ready for those events, we must view the end of our world, as described by His true prophets. After all, God has promised us, "Surely the Lord God will do nothing, but he revealeth his secrets unto his servants the prophets" (Amos 3:7).

The prophet Isaiah describes the end of our world in detail. Imagine this scene; it is soon to happen:

"Behold, the Lord maketh the earth empty, and maketh it waste, and turneth it upside down, and scattereth abroad the inhabitants thereof....The land shall be utterly emptied, and utterly spoiled: for the Lord hath spoken this word. The earth mourneth and fadeth away, the world languisheth and fadeth away, the haughty people of the earth do languish. The earth also is defiled under the inhabitants thereof; ***because*** *they have* ***transgressed*** *the* ***laws***, ***changed*** *the* ***ordinance***, ***broken*** *the everlasting* ***covenant***. **Therefore** hath the curse devoured the earth, and they that dwell therein are desolate: **therefore** the inhabitants of the earth are burned, and few men left" (Isaiah 24:1,3-6, emphasis supplied).

We are saved by grace. We cannot add any merit to what Jesus did for us with His precious blood. But the Bible makes it too clear to miss, that when human beings in their finite wisdom attempt to change God's holy law, they are bringing down the very curse of God upon themselves. Note the three reasons God gives for the final destruction of the earth. The inhabitants have:

1. "Transgressed the laws." Do people today transgress God's laws? More than ever before. Just look around our world and witness the stealing, killing, immorality, sacrilege, adultery, and every other sin condemned by God's laws being committed on a wholesale level. And in the Sermon on the Mount, Jesus made it clear that we really sin in our minds long before we actually commit the act (see Matthew 5). Pride, self-righteousness, lust, unbelief, impatience, hate, and selfishness in all its forms are just as sinful as any act we may see on the evening news. "The Lord looketh on the heart" (1 Samuel 16:7). Even if we break just one of His Commandments, we have in essence broken them all (see James 2:10).

2. "Changed the ordinance." Have humans today tried to change an ordinance of God? Most definitely. This was happening even in Christ's day. He said to the Pharisees, who claimed to be promoting and keeping God's laws, "Thus have ye made the **commandment of God** of none effect **by your tradition**." He also made it quite clear that they were "teaching for doctrines the **commandments of men**" (Matthew 15:6,9).

The same exact problem that Christ pointed out, Isaiah said would happen just before the end of the world. Have the traditions of this world caused you to forget or neglect God's laws, which He specifically told us to "Remember" (Exodus 20:8)? Traditions are fine as long as they do not replace the Word and will of our Creator. This type of attempt to alter the Ten Commandments is what we should watch for in these last days.

3. "Broken the everlasting covenant." What *is* the everlasting covenant? All we have to go by is the Word of God. Let's let the Bible interpret itself.

An angel is described in Revelation 14 as proclaiming the "everlasting gospel" to "every nation, and kindred, and tongue, and people" that "dwell on the earth" (Rev. 14:6). The next angel proclaims the fall of "Babylon," and the third angel warns the earth of the Beast, his image, and his mark (verses 8-10). So we see that the everlasting gospel (which is really God's covenant with those who have faith in Him) is tied inseparably to this proclamation that Babylon is fallen, and these warnings about the Beast and his mark. Don't miss that point. Now when we look down at verse 12 we see a picture of those who do not receive this "mark" of the Beast: "Here is the patience of the saints: here are they that **keep the commandments of God**, and the **faith of Jesus**."

As we take the words of Isaiah's vision of the end, and place them beside these final three messages that God is sending to the world, it becomes very clear that the coming Beast power will have but one goal in mind: to somehow make human traditions alter the law of God. This is going on right now all around us, but when pressure comes to enforce these traditions upon people, then we can know that Isaiah 24 is starting to unfold.

Remember, the Lord showed Isaiah that the specific *reason* the earth will be made desolate is because the "everlasting covenant" would be broken by humans. The best definition of that covenant will not be found in most "Armageddon" and "Antichrist" books that are circulating today. It will be found in the New Testament:

"This is the **covenant** that I will make with them after those days, saith the Lord, **I will put my laws into their hearts, and in their minds will I write them**" (Hebrews 10:16).

Reader, please do not allow yourself to be tossed to and fro by every wind of doctrine. Don't look for a mystery man to arise in the Middle East and take over the world with his tattoo machine. Don't wait for a microchip to be secretly implanted into an unwary population. Do not speculate as to the power of some super computer in Europe that will enforce the Mark of the Beast. No, rather look inside your own heart and ask the Lord to take control of it. Ask Him to clean out any of the things inside that are not in harmony with His will. Only allow Him to write that everlasting covenant within your heart and mind—to put His perfect law there—and you will be safe from the storm that is soon to break upon humanity. Ask yourself this, and be honest with yourself: Is there anything that I am doing in my spiritual walk with God that conflicts with His Commandments, and which can be supported by nothing more than the "traditions of men"? Examine the Ten Commandments prayerfully. Read them through very carefully. The Holy Spirit will guide you as you seek to know His will, for we have been promised that He will lead us "into all truth" (John 16:13).

❖ ❖ ❖

You have studied God's unchanging Word and you know all about last day events. Long have you waited for the fulfillment of these prophecies, for you know that when these things take place, the end "is near, even at the doors" (Matt. 24:33).

You see increasing trouble coming upon the world in crime, pollution, natural disasters, wars, and rumors of wars. The world's attention seems to be focused more and more on finding a solution to the problem. Many who recognize the problem as a *moral* one, mistakenly propose a *legal* solution. Instead of calling on a confused and dying world to turn to God and ask Him for a new heart (Ezekiel 36:26), the religious leaders work to influence the government and its laws. The growing number of crises have bound the world into a tighter and tighter snare of apparent helplessness, and those in authority seem to be increasingly willing to resort to drastic measures.

You have seen the civil rights of the people rapidly decrease, and yet, like the Pharisees against Christ, persecution has been promoted in the name of religion. The end, it has been reported, will surely justify the means, for we as a nation must get back to God and regain His favor. Just as Jesus predicted, they blindly "think that [they] doeth God a service" (John 16:2) as they oppress those who do not see things their way.

This erroneous view of God reaches its climax in the enforcement of laws which dictate the observance of Christian traditions—traditions which cannot be found in the Word of God, but which, as in the days of the Pharisees, have supplanted God's Word. You know that even if these new laws *were* in harmony with Bible standards, the very fact that they are being forced on people is contrary to the ways of the Savior. You have spent time with Him daily in prayer and Bible study, and you have grown to know Him as a God who wants our service and obedience to be a response of love, not fear of retribution.

Your favorite newscaster announces that according to expert sources, these new laws will be difficult to enforce, and that they really are just a symbolic gesture, sure to be left as a technicality on the law books. But you know better. The Bible has told you where this is headed.

You are amazed at the lack of concern by your fellow believers. Many of them have also known about these events in prophecy, and in fact have proclaimed them to the world. But for some reason they have not remained true to the message, and now they brush this news report off as "no big deal." Some of them even support the new measure. You remember the words of Christ that "brother shall deliver up the brother to death, and the father the child: and the children shall rise up against their parents, and cause them to be put to death. And ye shall be hated of all men for my name's sake: but he that endureth to the end shall be saved" (Matt. 10:21,22).

And what brings all of this about? You get out your Bible again and re-read Isaiah 24, Exodus 20, Revelation 13 & 14, and many of the other passages that you have learned. A decision *must* be made. Will you go along with these new laws, or will you stand upon the Word of God? No thoughts of rebellion come to mind, no plans of stockpiling weapons. These are the tactics of the fearful, and you have implicit faith in the protective power of your Father alone. You have no fear of this world, because "love casteth out fear" (1 John 4:18). Your love for and friendship with God, along with submission to His will, have cast out all fear of anything that can come to you now. Like the three Hebrews facing the fiery furnace, you do not concern yourself so much with your own well-being as with the glorification of your heavenly Father, and the holiness of His will.

A peace that passes all understanding fills your soul as you stand by your daily commitment to put God above everything else. Come what may, and with no retaliation on your part, you rest assured in the providence of your Father. Like Daniel asleep in the lions' den you have committed your soul into the hands of your Lord. You trust that where to go and what to do will now be made plain to you as He sees fit. In prayer you thank God for the lifesaving truths that have been revealed in His Word. You humbly realize that the only reason you can make this decision to put His will first is because of the strength that He supplies. Had you put off your relationship with Him, this moment would have had a far different outcome. Your actions would then be prompted by fear and self-preservation instead of love and trust in God. Thankfully, graciously, the Lord has exercised your faith daily for quite some time now so that it would be prepared for this final conflict.

An emotional tug of war takes place within you. Your heart is heavy with sorrow for those who have chosen blindness and the traditions of men over God's Word. At the same time you have peace from the throne of God, and excitement and joy because the end is indeed near. The moment for which you have so long waited is about to take place. Soon you will see Jesus face to face, and share in His fellowship forevermore. Soon you will declare with the great multitude of the redeemed those words so long anticipated:

"Lo, this is our God; we have waited for him; and he will save us: this is the Lord; we have waited for him, we will be glad and rejoice in his salvation!" (Isaiah 25:9).

"I am come that they might have life, and that they might have it more abundantly." —John 10:10

"Thou wilt shew me the path of life: in thy presence is fulness of joy; at thy right hand there are pleasures for evermore."
—Psalm 16:11

There are two great misconceptions about heaven. On the one hand there's the idea that its source of joy will be the mansions, material possessions, and other such things. On the other hand is the notion that it will be a boring place, void of all of the "fun" things in life. Those who think of heaven strictly in terms of gold and mansions need to spend far more time at the foot of the Cross. Those who feel it will be boring need to do their research. For the Bible promises that our future home will indeed be a place so full of joy and adventure that it will bring us "pleasures for evermore."

Our finite minds cannot even begin to grasp the countless blessings that await our discovery. What will that first trip from earth to heaven really be like? Will we go directly there, or will we stop off at distant galaxies along the way? What about the fact that Jesus said He would grant the overcomers to actually sit with Him on His throne (Revelation 3:21)? Such undeserved blessings! Will any new life forms be created after we get to heaven, and if so, imagine the stories we will have to tell them! These beings will have never heard about the great rebellion which started eons ago in the heart of a mighty angel: a rebellion in which we have all shared a part. Imagine explaining to them that you were once on the side of that Prince of Darkness, but were saved and re-created by the Prince of Peace.

Jesus promises to give every one of the redeemed a "white stone" inscribed with their new name (Revelation 2:17). What do you suppose that white stone looks like? What is its purpose? What new name has Christ chosen for you? The Savior also promised to give a "crown of life" to those who "love him," and are "faithful unto death" (James 1:12; Revelation 2:10; see also 1 Corinthians 9:25; 2 Timothy 4:8; 1 Peter 5:4). In the presence of the King of kings, however, the redeemed will no doubt cast them at the foot of His throne as did the "24 elders" in John's vision (Revelation 4:10). And the song that only the 144,000 can learn (Revelation 14:3), what will it sound like? So many things to contemplate. So many things to look forward to.

Physical activity and stimulation will be a constant blessing to the redeemed. The tending of the land will forever provide a peaceful contentment. The projects undertaken will exercise and strengthen every physical and mental faculty. Architectural endeavors planned and completed under the blessing of the Savior, will perpetually provide new and exciting challenges.

Perhaps you are one of those thrill seekers, who will try anything. You've never known thrills until you have scaled the peaks of distant worlds that dwarf a thousand Jupiters, or plunged down blue sky rivers which cascade from cloud to cloud. You've lived a sheltered life until you have navigated caves which trail to the very core of a world, or perched atop a distant sun after riding the crest of a solar flare.

In addition to all of the physical activities, there is an exhaustless array of studies to engage the mental powers. The human mind was created to derive pleasure from learning and discovering new things. This is why humans invent things. It is why we are fascinated by the latest technological advances. It's why we like watching the evening news, and why we love to travel. We are an inquisitive people: constantly seeking, constantly discovering. There is just something about the quest for knowledge, even if only for curiosity's sake, that intrigues the human soul.

Endless are the interests which can be pursued in the world to come. Is music your passion? We haven't even begun to understand all of the facets of this wonderful gift, or the intimate ways it affects the human soul. Perhaps astronomy is your thing. The wonders of the universe lie always before you. Are black holes real, and if so, what's it really like to explore one? A recent set of pictures from the Hubble telescope revealed, among other things, a huge, cloud-like pillar in space which measured around 1 trillion miles from top to bottom. Our entire earth would be but a speck in such an enormous object. The boundless expanse of the universe contains endless secrets for your continual discovery. Maybe you're enthralled by nature. Even in this old world there are animals in the deepest parts of the ocean that have rarely, if ever, been seen by humans. In the new earth, what else will we uncover? Firsthand, you'll be able to observe and explore every intricate detail and function of plant and animal life, the Creator Himself blessing you with thrilling insights. And what about the molecular elements? Consider all of the amazing advances that have already been made through molecular engineering. One look at the science that was behind the atom bomb and you realize that there are secrets still out there, the discoveries of which can unleash a torrent of power. What other forces are lying dormant, just waiting to be tapped?

And yet in spite of how satisfying and enlightening these studies will be in themselves, all sciences will ultimately point the student to the love and power of God. The Creator's name is written upon every tree and flower, upon the lofty mountain and the humble insect, upon the largest planet and tiniest atom. His signature of wisdom can be found on everything which came forth from His hand. As His creative authorship is thus revealed, it will magnify His power to re-create as well. And nowhere was that power more clearly revealed than at Calvary. There mankind, by beholding such selfless love, might be changed into the same image. The science of all sciences is and ever will be the Cross. The Sacrifice on Calvary will be the study that brings forth our deepest fulfillment and highest praise. It is the ultimate level of knowledge ever to be attained. And yet eternity itself is not enough time to unlock all of its mysteries. As we investigate this glorious truth we will see that our redemption involved far more than we understood on the surface.

Many Christians today feel that once they have read the crucifixion account in the Bible they have learned all there is to know. They assume that there are no more treasures to be gleaned from the mystery of such infinite condescension on our behalf. Yet even now there are diligent souls who have grasped the fact that Calvary constantly presents new truths—indeed new layers of truth—to those who are willing to search. How much more will be uncovered by minds changed to perfection at the Second Coming of Christ?

As the years roll by, your greatest pastime will be hearing of this redemptive love from the Master Himself. Learning more about the great controversy between Christ and Satan, which brought about the wonderful Plan to save your soul, will lead to an overwhelming desire to simply abide in His company. As you thus spend time in His presence, you will discover that it provides the greatest joy in the universe. So it can be today. Our quiet time with Him now can become the best time of the day. Our highest joy can be found in loving Him. We can get to the place where we no longer have a rushed personal worship time, but commune with Him as our Best Friend and Father. Those who spend time with Him here and now will be dwelling in His presence there and then. By beholding Him day by day, we will become like Him in word and deed. We will live as He lived, and love as He loved.

May you come to know by experience the fullness of joy that is found in His presence today, and for all eternity, at His right hand, share in those pleasures forevermore.

❖ ❖ ❖

It is time for your favorite journey. Millions of golden trumpets herald the event. The angels themselves wield these horns atop the jasper walls of the Holy City. What is this glorious event? The Son of God is going to visit the outer reaches of His universe, and He is taking you with Him. As one who was "redeemed from among men"—alive at the Second Coming and translated to heaven without seeing death—you are among those who "follow the Lamb withersoever he goeth" (Revelation 14:3,4). During the eleventh hour of earth's history you had shared in the trials of those who lived through the "time of trouble such as never was since there was a nation" (Daniel

12:1). By the blood of the Lamb, you overcame the Beast power and did not receive his mark. Thus on this day, you and the rest of the 144,000 accompany Christ on His journey. Thus you can sing a special song; "and no man could learn that song but the hundred and forty and four thousand, which were redeemed from the earth" (Revelation 14:3).

Now you and the others in this group begin to sing the "song of Moses the servant of God, and the song of the Lamb" (Revelation 15:3). True to prophecy, this song can only be sung by you and the others who were translated at the very end. It is a song about your unique experience: a song about the seemingly impossible victory that is available through Christ, when He is formed within. This song glorifies Jesus and declares to the endless universe that fallen human beings had no righteousness and no power within themselves, and that their only hope was through the crucifixion of the Holy One.

And oh, how you love this song. It swells as earth's last generation streams into the city for the voyage. With each uplifted voice the song moves closer to its climax, yet it will not end until all have arrived for the journey. From near and far they approach the King. Some were already in the city, while others are returning from distant galaxies. All have the majestic chorus on their lips. Every singer has a unique part in this magnificent song. As the Savior listens to the hymn of praise, He knows if a single voice is missing. He can also tell just by looking at the growing throng when it has reached its specific number. So intimate is His relationship with every one of you! So special is each soul to His heart! His face reveals His boundless love, surpassing any father's love for his children, as you all continue to gather around Him.

You wonder where you're going this time, as you wait for the group to assemble. Jesus does not map out all of His plans for you, and that's just the way you like it. You know that wherever He takes you, it will be filled with wonderful surprises and new, glorious revelations of His omnipotence and character. In past journeys you have watched Him create colossal new suns. You have seen quasars ignite at His command, and nebulas called forth from nothingness. You have accompanied Him from world to world across the distant galaxies as He blessed the inhabitants therein.

Your own life has been blessed in infinite ways since the first day you gave yourself to Him. You have experienced "the mystery which hath been hid from ages and from generations" (Colossians 1:26): that mystery being "Christ in you, the hope of glory" (verse 27). To have the Savior living His life in you by the Holy Spirit is the highest honor ever bestowed upon created beings. Just to be in His presence provides a fullness of joy beyond anything you ever dreamed possible. He is the Life-giver, the sustaining power for everything that exists in the entire universe. You admire and love His character. You follow Him wherever He goes.

Here in this place of eternal glory, you have contemplated with endless delight the magnificence of both creative power and redeeming love. All of your faculties have been enlarged and exercised as you have undertaken new challenges of intellect and imagination. Spiritual, physical, and mental capacities are continually increasing by the grace of God. The secrets of the sciences, so long kept hidden from the wisest of earthlings, are now open to your mind as you search the wonders of the universe. Your highest ambitions have been reached, and yet with each advance in knowledge new heights are presented and surmounted. Boredom has been forever blotted from existence as the science of God's love and power unfolds before you.

You stand at the center of the universe, beholding the Source of all life. The endless galaxies and solar systems follow their appointed paths circling the great throne of the Infinite One: the one Light that outshines all of the suns combined. In His presence all else seems to disappear. At times such as these it is just you and Him, child and Father, engulfed by an energy of love that surpasses all understanding. To experience this love is all that matters. To truly know God is indeed eternal life (John 17:3).

The last of the assembly have arrived. The song of Moses and the Lamb reaches its climax and the final note includes every voice. All kneel in the presence of the Lamb. Silence surrounds the Savior, but soon His powerful, deep voice pronounces a blessing upon the group. There is power in those words, and your very being seems to be charged with new energy. All now rise, eager to behold Him yet again as He speaks into existence the cloud which will transport you into the great beyond.

A fine, white mist begins to form, and slowly swirls around the throng as it grows. The City rumbles below as the power of God begins to lift the entire mass off the glistening surface. An awesome wind churns the air around you loudly. It sounds like a hundred hurricanes. Chills dance along your spine as you experience this mighty force. You look down and the cloud is bubbling, yet firm beneath your feet. In the spaces that open and close, your eyes catch the fire that has ignited under its base. The New Jerusalem now shines far beneath you. The cloud accelerates as it enters the outer limits of the atmosphere and now the earth itself begins to shrink.

These cosmic expeditions always remind you of your first incredible journey with Him so many millennia ago: the journey that rescued you from a dying planet called Earth, and ushered you into that "exceeding good land" called Heaven. Although ages upon ages have since rolled by, your memory of that first trip has never dimmed. Your love for the Savior has only grown as your knowledge of Him has increased.

Your eyes gaze upon the One who took your place on Calvary, and you rejoice in the truth of what He did and who He is. The greatest thing about forever is the fact that it will be spent with Him. You wonder in amazement how anyone in the old earth could have doubted such love. He is everything to you. You have found Him to be just what the Scriptures always declared Him to be: "the Cheifest among ten thousand," "the Desire of all nations," and "the One altogether lovely."

As the massive cloud moves through the cosmos, your anticipation grows. What glorious destination awaits you this time? What fresh displays of creative power will be exhibited on this trip? You take one more glance back as the New Earth fades from view. Only the light of Glory can be seen among the stars. Amidst that light is your real home, the place where Jesus reigns.

You actually live in that better land, so long spoken of, so long hoped for. Made from the hand of God, it cannot help but be true, lovely, and pure. How great is the love that God has for you! For endless ages to come you will contemplate this love. Throughout all eternity you will think on these things.

Spending eternity with Jesus is the greatest gift that will ever be offered to you. Nothing is worth forfeiting that experience. "For what is a man profited, if he shall gain the whole world, and lose his own soul? or what shall a man give in exchange for his soul?" (Matthew 16:26).

Appreciation for anything grows with our familiarity with it. This is also true in our relationship with the Lord. Think about eternal realities often. Think about the Cross even more often. Slow down and spend some time at least once a week out in nature, God's glorious creation, examining the handiwork of the Master Designer. If you don't have easy access to such a place, then take some time to enjoy the incredible view that God has given to all parts of the world: look up into the canopy of stars at night, and contemplate the Creator of them all. It may seem like a small thing, but it truly makes a difference. In this steel and concrete world, our bond with nature is breaking. A great blessing awaits those who would restore that bond. Many portions of this book were written after morning walks out in nature, where the trees, the birds, and the flowers brought to mind the eternal springtime of the land that awaits the children of God. It is a real land. Just as real as any place you have ever visited.

You have spent some significant time now reading and thinking about God and heavenly things. Never forget that the Lord thinks about you, too. His thoughts are on you every day. His love for you, His concern over things that frustrate you, His plans for your life, and all the things He longs to do with you as you spend eternity together: these are the things that fill His mind.

"But I am poor and needy; **yet the Lord thinketh upon me**: thou art my help and my deliverer," "How precious also are thy thoughts unto me, O God! How great is the sum of them!", "Many, O Lord my God, are thy wonderful works which thou hast done, and thy thoughts which are to us-ward: they cannot be reckoned up in order unto thee: **if I would declare and speak of them, they are more than can be numbered**" (Psalm 40:17; 139:17; 40:5).

God's thoughts toward you are more than can be numbered! You are not just a statistic; you are His son, His daughter. He thinks about you every moment. He is thinking of you right now. Give yourself to the One who gave Himself for you.

Life in this world is so temporary; it's all soon to pass away. In comparison to eternity, your life on this planet is but a split second. Your angel will probably come up to you one day in the New Jerusalem and tell you that your time in heaven has just equaled your entire life span on earth. Yet it won't seem possible. You'll feel as though you just got there. And still an eternity of increasing joy awaits you. Someone once said that true life begins after the Second Coming; our existence today is really just stepping up to the starting line. Where will you be in a billion years from this moment? There are only three votes cast for your eternal destiny. God always votes for you to be saved and Satan always votes for you to be lost. Only you can cast the deciding vote. That vote means surrendering all to your Savior. Satan can never force the will, and God won't. He loved your freedom of choice so much He decided it would be better to have His own Son suffer an ignominious death on the Cross, than to take away your free will. Exercise that will by giving yourself to Him today.

It has been my wish that all who have had enough interest in heaven to read this book would come to a knowledge of the boundless love that was manifested on the Cross of Calvary. I have hoped and prayed that the words on these pages would bring the love of Jesus into clear view for those who may have gotten lost in the fog.

Friend, have you accepted Him as your Savior? You can do it this very minute—right now. Do you want to get to know Him on an intimate level? You can begin a new, life-changing relationship today. His hand is outstretched just waiting to pull you up out of the mire of sin. Perhaps you once knew the Lord, but the cares of this world, or maybe some painful trials, have pulled you away. Perhaps you have failed so many times in your spiritual walk that you are ready to throw in the towel. Do believe He is still on your side. Do trust in the One who longs to forgive and delights in mercy. Come to Him now, and determine to spend more time with Him than ever before. He *will* change your heart. You *will be* a new creature. The Creator has promised.

May the Lord bless you in your daily walk with Him, and may the God of peace sanctify you wholly, so that with the apostle Paul you can proclaim for all eternity "I count all things but loss for the excellency of the knowledge of Christ Jesus my Lord" (Philippians 3:8).

ABOUT THE AUTHOR

Carl Martin wrote his first poem, "Jesus," in the fourth grade, and has been writing ever since. Immediately after his high school graduation in 1986, he took a prodigal journey away from both his home town and his spiritual life. He moved to southern California in pursuit of a career in the entertainment industry. There he studied screenwriting and acting, and eventually landed an agent. But in the summer of 1993 God opened his eyes and he realized just how much he needed the Lord. He then dedicated his life and abilities to serving Christ, and spreading the good news of the Gospel. Carl now works as a freelance writer and outreach coordinator in southern California, and has spoken at various churches. He is 32 years old and lives in the small town of Agua Dulce, located in the hills just north of Los Angeles. His home is shared by his wife Coleen, his 3-year-old son Daltry, and their dog Rocky. Carl has a burden to tell as many people as he can about the soon coming of the Lord Jesus Christ. If you would like to drop a line to Carl, contact the publishers or email him directly at *Writecarl@Hotmail.com.*

Send a *HEAVEN*-ly Gift! (*details below)

To order additional copies of ***HEAVEN, Think On These Things*** please complete the following order form:

Ship to:____
Address:____
City, State, Zip____
Day Phone____

____ This is a gift (see below)

____ copies of *HEAVEN, Think On These Things*

@ $10.95 each $______
Shipping @ $2.00 first book + 75¢ each additional book $______
CA residents add 8.25% sales tax $______
Total amount enclosed $______

Make checks payable to ***Total Grace Publications***

Send to: Total Grace Publications
28010 N. Tiffany Ln. #302
Santa Clarita, CA 91351

Or visit our web site and **order on-line** at **www.totalgrace.com**

*Books are always great gift ideas. TGP will be glad to ship a gift-wrapped copy of this book to your specified recipient, complete with a card and message from you, at no extra charge. Just write your message below:

____
____
____
____

DISCOVER

Boundless Freedom...
Endless Joy

DISCOVER
answers from the source you
can trust: the Bible.
This is your opportunity
to find answers to the questions
that affect your life and happiness
— absolutely FREE —
in the 26 beautifully illustrated
Discover Bible Guides.

Yes! Please send my **FREE** *Discover Bible Guides* today. I want to discover God's answers to life's greatest questions. I understand all 26 of the *Discover Guides* are **FREE**.

Name____
Address____
City____________________________State________Zip_______________

Please clip and mail this completed coupon to:

DISCOVER, Box 55
Los Angeles, CA 90053-0055